Eliminativism in Ancient Philosophy

Also available from Bloomsbury:

Atomism in Philosophy, edited by Ugo Zilioli
Beyond Hellenistic Epistemology, by Charles E. Snyder
Nietzsche's Renewal of Ancient Ethics, by Neil Durrant
The Metaphysics of Existence and Nonexistence, by Matthew Davidson
Wittgenstein and the Problem of Metaphysics, by Michael Smith

Eliminativism in Ancient Philosophy

Greek and Buddhist Philosophers on Material Objects

Ugo Zilioli

BLOOMSBURY ACADEMIC
LONDON • NEW YORK • OXFORD • NEW DELHI • SYDNEY

BLOOMSBURY ACADEMIC
Bloomsbury Publishing Plc, 50 Bedford Square, London, WC1B 3DP, UK
Bloomsbury Publishing Inc, 1385 Broadway, New York, NY 10018, USA
Bloomsbury Publishing Ireland, 29 Earlsfort Terrace, Dublin 2, D02 AY28, Ireland

BLOOMSBURY, BLOOMSBURY ACADEMIC and the Diana logo
are trademarks of Bloomsbury Publishing Plc

First published in Great Britain 2024
This paperback edition published 2025

Copyright © Ugo Zilioli, 2024

Ugo Zilioli has asserted his right under the Copyright, Designs and
Patents Act, 1988, to be identified as Author of this work.

For legal purposes the Preface and Acknowledgements on pp. vi–viii constitute
an extension of this copyright page.

Cover image: Sri Lanka: Frieze of musicians, Isurumuniya temple
museum, Anuradhapura. Isurumuniya Vihara is a rock temple built
during the reign of King Devanampiya Tissa (r. 307 – 267 BCE)
CPA Media Pte Ltd / Alamy Stock Photo

All rights reserved. No part of this publication may be: i) reproduced or transmitted in any form, electronic or mechanical, including photocopying, recording or by means of any information storage or retrieval system without prior permission in writing from the publishers; or ii) used or reproduced in any way for the training, development or operation of artificial intelligence (AI) technologies, including generative AI technologies. The rights holders expressly reserve this publication from the text and data mining exception as per Article 4(3) of the Digital Single Market Directive (EU) 2019/790.

Bloomsbury Publishing Inc does not have any control over, or responsibility for, any third-party websites referred to or in this book. All internet addresses given in this book were correct at the time of going to press. The author and publisher regret any inconvenience caused if addresses have changed or sites have ceased to exist, but can accept no responsibility for any such changes.

A catalogue record for this book is available from the British Library.

ISBN:	HB:	978-1-3501-0516-4
	PB:	978-1-3504-0085-6
	ePDF:	978-1-3501-0517-1
	eBook:	978-1-3501-0518-8

Typeset by Integra Software Services Pvt. Ltd.

For product safety related questions contact productsafety@bloomsbury.com.

To find out more about our authors and books visit www.bloomsbury.com
and sign up for our newsletters.

Contents

Preface and acknowledgements — vi

Introduction: Nothing for us? — 1

1. Protagoras' Secret Doctrine: An exercise in ancient eliminativism — 13
2. Twins and dharmas. Protagoras and Vasubandhu on a two-tier ontology of tropes — 29
3. Gorgias and Nāgārjuna on nihilism — 47
4. On things. The origin and genealogy of Pyrrho's metaphysics — 65
5. The Cyrenaics on indeterminacy — 83
6. The Cyrenaics on solipsism and privacy — 101

Conclusion: Eliminativism, indeterminacy and nihilism between East and West — 119

Notes — 126
References — 155
Index — 165

Preface and acknowledgements

This book has been long in the making, since I conceived the first initial idea about it a decade ago. It brings together some different, yet converging strands of my research into a unified whole. The book as it stands has been written in the last two years under the auspices of a Leverhulme Grant (Leverhulme Research Grant RPG-2021-204) that has provided me, among many other things, with the freedom to pursue my research with no other academic obligations. I really wish to thank the Trust for its generous support and for the overall stimulus it offers to the Humanities in general.

Over the years, many colleagues and friends have read or commented on some parts of what has now become this book. I thus wish to thank the following people: Diego Zucca, Roberta Ioli, Matthew Duncombe, Voula Tsouna, Joachim Aufderheide, Livio Rossetti, Tim O'Keefe, Richard Bett, Aldo Brancacci, Kurt Lampe, Francesco Verde, Robin Hendry, Matthew Tugby, Pedro Mesquita and Mikolaj Domaradzki. I also thank audiences at Oxford, Lisbon and Ascea for discussions and oral feedback. Amber Carpenter and I started talking about Buddhist philosophy in 2017 in Durham, during a conference on atomism that I organized. Since then, she has been a helpful, supportive and congenial colleague to talk on all things Greek and Buddhist. More than any others, I owe a great debt of gratitude for Jan Westerhoff, with whom I am carrying out the Leverhulme project on Greek and Buddhist philosophers I have mentioned above. His acumen of mind, generosity of spirit and tactful manners make him the ideal colleague any academic dreams of. I thank him for being there all the time, with his help, comments, encouragement and inspiration for further, new paths in my research. Chris Gill has not read this last manuscript but since I met him twenty years ago as my PhD external examiner he has been to me, and still is nowadays, a model of academic mentorship, human integrity and philosophical excellence. I thank him for his constant support.

True to its fame, Oxford University has proven to be the best among academic settings for carrying out my research. The newly established Oxford

Network of Ancient philosophy, under the directorship of Ursula Coope, gathers specialists in the whole spectrum of ancient philosophy, East and West and is thus a congenial venue to discuss comparative philosophy. Thanks to all involved for their support and feedback. The Faculty of Theology and Religion is a great place to work and I wish to thank all the staff there, in particular, Lisa Driver Davidson for her efficiency and professionalism.

Once again, people at Bloomsbury Academic are the best publishing team any scholar or indeed writer can dream of. Colleen Coalter is the best of editors, always patient, encouraging, tolerant and imaginative. Suzie Nash has handled the whole process, from the initial proposal to the final stages of the submission, with care, efficiency and support. Thank you very much to you both. While providing a detailed feedback on the whole manuscript, the Reviewer for the Press has greatly helped me to reshape some of my arguments in a more convincing way as well as to tighten the overall structure of the book and the balance between chapters. I hope this now reflects in the book and s/he is pleased about it. I also wish to thank Benedict O'Hagan at Bloomsbury and Ayyan Ejilane (and his team) at Integra for their work in preparing the manuscript for the publication.

Special thanks are also due to people at Barefoot Cafe in North Parade and at IScream at the Covered Market, both in Oxford, for providing me with excellent coffee and ice cream, and for their interest in my work.

As any writer knows well, writing is an exciting and rewarding experience but also one that is time-consuming and very laborious. I have been greatly helped in the process by the company, affection and devotion of someone who is not a human being: our Persian cat, Eros. Our 'static' walks every morning with him on the leash have allowed me to clear my mind before returning afresh to the book (without moving much, he is happy to sniff around and look at trees and birds with me on his side); his calm, yet talking presence next to me all the time when I work from home is a reassuring reminder of how much the emotional balance of human beings owes to affectionate pets. He will not be able to read these words but I am sure he knows how grateful I am to him.

Finally, this book has only been made possible by the love and unwavering support of my family. My daughter Zoe and my son Delio have always followed me in the different directions that my academic career has taken us to go, always putting up a smiling face when the changes and the challenges were difficult to handle, always brimming with life, laughter and courage. From afar geographically, but never emotionally, I always felt my best friend of more than forty-five years Michele next to me all the time, supporting, encouraging, understanding, helping in all the ways that only a prolonged friendship such ours can know. My wife Cristiana has been the bedrock of my life since I fell in love with her at first sight more than twenty-three years ago. There has been no day in our emotionally rich and immensely rewarding life together in which our love has been less than magnificent. I get up every morning with the confidence that with her, it will be another day full of happiness, joy, dialogue and new shared plans for our future. To her this book is dedicated, with much love.

Cannon Court/Casa di Margherita
Oxford/Colmurano, July 2023

Introduction: Nothing for us?

This book is about eliminativism in ancient philosophy: Greek and Buddhist. To give an initial framework of reference that could help readers navigating the material with some ease, let me say something about eliminativism first, and then about the ancient philosophers who are to be dealt with in the following pages.

Ontological eliminativism

The kind of eliminativism that is the main topic of this book is ontological eliminativism, that is, eliminativism about material objects.[1] In the next pages and throughout the whole book, I shall be focusing on some philosophers who for different reasons and scope do away with material objects. In the context of the present monograph, eliminativism is a label that has to be taken in a rather broad sense in so long as it is able to capture under the same conceptual umbrella a variety of cognate views about material objects that were circulating in ancient philosophy. Some Greek philosophers such as Protagoras (at least in the context of the first part of Plato's *Theaetetus*) eliminate material objects in so far as they make them wholly replaceable by processes and by an ontology of property-particulars. Other Greek philosophers such as Pyrrho elaborate a metaphysical view of the world as ultimately undifferentiated, unstable and indeterminate. In this way, material objects appear to be still there at first sight, but their nature is such that they are ultimately eliminated as determinate, ontologically stable items of the material world, or indeed eliminated tout court.[2] In another case, that of the Cyrenaics, in contrast with much recent scholarship, I aim to show that this important Socratic and post-Socratic school may have endorsed a metaphysical outlook that makes material objects wholly elusive and ontologically redundant. Lastly, I make a bold case to take Gorgias' first claim that nothing is in his work *What Is Not or On Nature* as a profession of ontological nihilism: nothing, including the material objects of our everyday life, is said by Gorgias to truly exist. Eliminativism has thus seemed to me the best metaphysical view, among those available, able to capture the conceptual similarities and theoretical affinities between those ancient doctrines that, although in different ways and with different purposes, aimed at eliminating material objects as stable, determinate and enduring items of the world.

Protagoras, Gorgias, Pyrrho, the Cyrenaics: these are the main Greek philosophers who are going to be dealt with in this book. On the interpretation I shall be offering in the context of the book, they endorse eliminativist ontologies that differ from, and contrast with, other more celebrated mainstream Greek ontologies, such as Plato's, Aristotle's or the Stoics'. Both ancient sources and contemporary studies have so far highlighted important philosophical connections between at least some of the Greek philosophers who are the main protagonists of this book. Ancient doxographers such as Diogenes Laertius, or Peripatetic philosophers such as Aristocles of Messene, or Epicurean enthusiasts such as Colotes of Lampsacus (as preserved in Plutarch) variously insisted on analogies and similarities between Protagoras, the Cyrenaics and Pyrrho; yet the nature and scope of their accounts were neither systematic nor free from biases dictated by different philosophical agendas. After all, their main interest in drawing connections between ancient philosophers or in sketching out the genealogy of a line of thought was mainly a critical one, that is, aimed at highlighting weaknesses in those doctrines as well as their implausibility from the standpoint of Aristotle's or Epicurus' views.[3] At the same time, closer to us in time, while it may be easy to find scholarly articles dealing with this or that aspect of alternative ontologies in ancient Greek thought, it is much harder to get a thorough account that explores the ontology of Greek eliminativism in a more comprehensive way. Despite it is *highly* plausible to read Protagoras and Pyrrho as committed to certain metaphysical views, despite it is possible to understand Gorgias and the Cyrenaics as committed to radical views about the material world,[4] very few scholars approach the question of what sort of metaphysical outlook all these thinkers may have endorsed. This book aims to fill, at least in part, this gap.

One may want to ask why ontological eliminativism in the first place. It is true that in the last decades, ontological eliminativism, again taken in a broad sense, has become a fashionable topic in contemporary metaphysics. Let us just think of the various attempts by Peter Unger, Peter Van Inwagen, Trenton Merricks and, more recently, by Jiri Benovsky to argue for different kinds of eliminativism about material objects (with Unger more back in time and Benovsky more recently endorsing an all-encompassing eliminativism about material objects and people).[5] At the same time, contemporary philosophers such as Jan Westerhoff, while drawing from the richness of Buddhist philosophy, have provided elaborate accounts of what it really means to be eliminativist or nihilist in metaphysics.[6]

My interest in eliminativism in ancient philosophy has however only been sparked by this more recent trend in contemporary debates. Such a recent trend has simply confirmed an idea that firstly came to my mind more than a decade ago, an idea that while working as an hermeneutical intuition, has pushed me to carry out a sort of a fairly systematic research on Protagoras, Gorgias, Pyrrho and the Cyrenaics under the hypothesis of ontological eliminativism. It is my claim in fact that a truly new understanding of ancient metaphysics is to be gained once we look at it under a new perspective.

We shall discover that in ancient Greek metaphysics there is a subterranean line of thought that challenges more orthodox ontologies by providing us with an alternative, eliminativist ontology. I say 'subterranean' not because we need to excavate deeply to see this line of thought emerging but simply because for a variety of reasons, we have so far not wanted to see it as we should have done if we really had aimed to depict the full richness of ancient Greek metaphysics in its extraordinary complexity. In Greek philosophy we have Plato and Aristotle, with an extended, literally captivating and philosophically developed evidence on their views (however disputable and disputed these views turn out to be when we try to reconstruct them). In addition, we have the great Hellenistic schools of the Stoics, Epicureans and Sceptics, with much less structured direct evidence, yet with a lot of indirect sources to rely on. This disparity in textual evidence gives all these well-known philosophers a great advantage point since it is somehow easier to get a firmer grip on their doctrines or views. On the contrary, when we deal with Protagoras, Gorgias, the Cyrenaics and Pyrrho, the situation changes drastically. Limited evidence and few sources push the scholar interested in their theories to work on a muddy and uneasy ground. Furthermore, the doctrines that these philosophers appear to hold (either Protagoras' relativism, or Gorgias' 'nihilist' views, or the Cyrenaics' subjectivism or Pyrrho's metaphysical indeterminacy) attracted a large amount of criticism already in the ancient world, so that these unorthodox doctrines seem already doomed to succumb under the strength of more powerful, more coherently reconstructed positions.

The combination of scanty evidence and unorthodoxy thus becomes lethal, relegating all these 'minor' philosophers into an area that is far from mainstream research. This is still the case nowadays, despite the really illuminating studies on these philosophers and their views that you will find quoted or referred to in the following pages. Yet, these are very original thinkers who were not only criticized in antiquity but also widely respected.[7] If one approaches them with care and patience, much is to be gained. More in particular, I claim that a synoptic analysis of Protagoras, Gorgias, Pyrrho and the Cyrenaics can reveal a line of eliminativist ontology that is truly worth looking at for its richness and diversity.

Partiality 1: Democritus and Heraclitus

The actual appreciation of the eliminativist ontologies of Protagoras, Gorgias, Pyrrho and the Cyrenaics is the first important step in a story that still needs to be told in full. This is still the case not only because no systematic attempt to deal with the ontologies of those philosophers has been so far fully carried out but also because there are other ancient Greek philosophers who can, at least on some reasonable interpretations, be inscribed into the line of ontological eliminativism that this book aims to reconstruct. On this respect, two names impose themselves: Heraclitus and Democritus. The former is the philosopher who famously insisted that the world is (in) flux, with nothing enduring in the vast array of processes that make up the thread of reality. In the Heraclitean world of processes, then, material objects do not seem to play a role at all. This is for instance clearly illustrated in the section of the *Theaetetus* that is under scrutiny in Chapters 1 and 2, where in conjunction and parallel with Protagoras' views, the Heracliteans are brought into discussion.

On his part, Democritus postulated atoms as the ultimate ontological elements of the material world.[8] This in itself makes composite material objects as wholly reducible to something more ontologically fundamental (that is, the atoms), again eliminating (macroscopic) things as we usually conceive of them from the world out there. Eliminativism is indeed one of the possible readings that the ancients gave to Democritean atomism, since Colotes' handling of Democritus does seem to point in that direction.[9] And if we share Plutarch's criticism of Colotes' handling of Democritus, it will be possible to argue that, despite the usual attribution to the Epicureans of a commonsensical view of the material world, Epicurean atomism too may be read as intrinsically linked to eliminativism.[10]

Partiality 2: Selfhood and personal identity

This book thus aims to be the first fairly systematic dealing with some unexplored ontologies in ancient philosophy, while especially focussing on ontological eliminativism. Yet, despite its novel approach, the book only remains a partial exploration of the richness and sophistication of ancient Greek eliminativism for two main reasons. First, however wide-ranging it could be, the book is not an exhaustive treatment of ancient eliminativism since it leaves out some relevant figures, such as Democritus and Heraclitus, who will make the appeal and diffusion of unorthodox ontologies in the context of ancient Greek philosophy more widespread than ever.[11]

There is also a second reason for which this book remains a partial attempt to deal with ancient eliminativism. In the following pages I am going to talk about material objects in general, with no distinction made for human beings. This is a distinction that needs to be carefully considered: human beings can well claim to have a different, special status among material objects. Human beings are equipped with a capacity to endure successive modifications, both physical and psychological, something that is completely lacking in other material objects. As briefly mentioned, contemporary attempts to defend eliminativism, such as Van Inwagen's and Merricks', offer an ontology of material objects where human beings and, more generally, living organisms are preserved as the only items admitted of.

In the scholarship on ancient Greek philosophy, there have recently been illuminating studies, such as those authored by Christopher Gill and Richard Sorabji, which have enormously advanced our understating of selfhood in Stoicism and, more in general, in ancient Greek philosophy.[12] Yet, once again, little has been done with reference to selfhood and personal identity in pre-Hellenistic thought, even less so regarding philosophers such as Protagoras, Gorgias, Pyrrho and the Cyrenaics (as well as Heraclitus and Democritus). This is due again to the problems about scanty evidence and philosophical minority I have referred to earlier. However, much can be done in this area, especially if we treat the topic of selfhood under the light of ontological eliminativism.

On the understanding I shall be offering in this book, Protagoras, Gorgias, Pyrrho and the Cyrenaics all endorse different forms of eliminativism about material objects. Some of these philosophers (such as Pyrrho) seem to make no exceptions for human beings; some others such as the Cyrenaics appear to make human beings as an exception to their eliminativism. Yet, the Cyrenaics can be claimed to endorse, at least on some interpretations, a conception of selfhood and personal identity that is not only similar to Parfit' reductionist view, but also one that has striking similarities with some positions to be found in the sophisticated debate on selfhood in Buddhist philosophy.[13]

In part III of *Reasons and Persons*, Parfit claims that what matters in the life of persons is not identity through time, but a sort of reduced psychological connectedness or continuity between different phases of what is (wrongly and traditionally) taken as one continuous self.[14] However revisionary his views on personal identity still are in contemporary Western philosophy,[15] Parfit is well aware that there are strong analogies between his view and the Buddha's view on persons. At one point, Parfit writes: 'As Appendix J shows, Buddha *would have agreed* [with Parfit's Reductionist View]. The Reductionist View is not merely part of one cultural tradition. It may be, as I have claimed, the true view about all people at all times' (Parfit 1987, p. 273).

While Parfit's claim may well be true, the Buddhist debate on selfhood and personal identity can claim with good reasons to be the most thorough and systematic attempt to understand personhood in the history of thought, both Western and Eastern. There are two important treatises on the refutation of personhood in Buddhism. One is Vasubandhu's *Refutation of the Theory of the Self*, which challenges the philosophical positions of a rival group of Buddhist thinkers, the Personalists. Another important refutation of traditional conceptions of selfhood in Buddhism is the one developed by Chandrakīrti, one of Nāgārjuna's finest commentators.[16] The Buddhist debate on personhood also produced the most sophisticated discussion on solipsism to be found in philosophy. In light of the conceptually rich discussion on selves and persons that dominated Buddhist debates on selfhood, two great Buddhist philosophers of the later generations, Dharmakīrti and Ratnakīrti, wrote two treatises discussing otherness and solipsism.[17]

This is an enormously exciting field to discover. There is much scope in exploring reductionist conceptions of selfhood and personal identity in ancient Greek and Buddhist philosophies in the context of eliminativist ontologies. Yet, a systematic account of reductionist views on selfhood in ancient philosophy, both Greek and Buddhist, is an ambitious project in itself and one that, it is hoped, will follow the present one. As far as persons are concerned, however, in this book I have to confine myself to dealing with the possible extent to which the Cyrenaics may have endorsed solipsism. Their eliminativism about material objects clashes with the importance they do recognize to the subject in both epistemological and ontological terms. It is worth asking whether, in contrast to the ontological elusiveness they attach to material objects, the Cyrenaics make the person (the subject) as the only truly existing items of their world.[18] It is thus illuminating to discuss their views on material objects in parallel with their position on selfhood and subjectivity. I do so in Chapter 6, when I deal with the possibility of solipsism in Cyrenaic thinking.

Buddhist philosophy

The partiality of my effort in the reconstruction of ontological eliminativism in ancient philosophy is hopefully counterbalanced not only by the fact that it is the first, fairly systematic attempt into that direction, but also by the other fact that some relevant discussions from Buddhist philosophy are well brought into the picture. It remains true that the main focus of the book is ancient

Greek philosophy, but it is also the case that two chapters of the book (that is, Chapters 2 and 3) offer what I hope will be an illuminating parallel between ancient Greek and Buddhist doctrines. I do so with reference to two Buddhist philosophers whose importance in the history of Buddhist thought is similar to that of Plato and Aristotle in ancient Greek philosophy: Vasubandhu and Nāgārjuna. In another chapter (Chapter 4), I tackle the issue of the origin and genealogy of Pyrrho's views, arguing that close analogies between his views and early Buddhism are there for us to appreciate. In the Conclusion I make further comments on the conceptual connections between eliminativism, indeterminacy and nihilism in both Greek and Buddhist philosophies. That three chapters of the book out of six deal also with Buddhist philosophy is, I hope, enough to justify the title of the book as an exploration of material objects in ancient philosophy, both Greek and Buddhist.

Why Buddhist philosophy, one may well ask. There is still much to do in scholarly terms in order to discover analogies and diversities between Greek and Buddhist philosophies. Both philosophies have attracted the interest of analytic philosophers who have been looking for inspiration in ancient philosophy, both Eastern and Western, to find compelling arguments in favour or against the theories they have been developing. But a comparative effort between Greek and Buddhist philosophies was limited, both in scope and diffusion, until the publication of Thomas McEvilley's *The Shape of Ancient Thought*, more than twenty years ago.[19] The book showed that it is indeed possible to gain a much deeper understanding of the ancient world if we approach ancient and Buddhist philosophers comparatively. The cultural temptation to take the two worlds of India and Greece as apart entities, with little in common, is somehow still dominant nowadays. But this is a wrong approach to take, and one that is being counterbalanced by a more positive outlook. The historical interchanges between Greece and India in pre-Hellenistic and Hellenistic times were much wider than one may initially expect;[20] it is these interchanges that are responsible for connections also at a broader, both cultural and philosophical level. In the context of human thought, the philosophical centrality of the West is an external, cultural superimposition, not something that is rooted in the history of both Greek and Buddhist societies. It is the actual removal of such a cultural superimposition that is opening up a new, exciting trend in comparative philosophy. After McEvilley's monumental effort, in more recent years there have been some important attempts to read Greek and Buddhist philosophies in a comparative way.[21] It is to this fairly new path in scholarship that this book too belongs.

This book

Let us have a brief look at the structure of this book. The first two chapters deal with Protagoras' Secret Doctrine as this is illustrated in Plato's *Theaetetus*. In the first part of the dialogue, that is, *Tht*. 151e–186a, after equating Theaetetus' first definition of knowledge as perception with Protagoras' man is the measure maxim, Socrates refers to a Secret Doctrine of Protagoras, something that he taught in secret to some well-chosen disciples. The first chapter, '*Protagoras' Secret Doctrine: An exercise in ancient eliminativism*', sets off the ground for an exploration of the main tenets of ancient Greek eliminativism by focusing on the main philosophical views and stages around which Protagoras' Secret Doctrine is centred and developed. This is an important first step in the appreciation of ancient eliminativism, since the philosophical views that are discussed in Protagoras' Secret Doctrine constitute an excellent introduction to the main doctrinal features of ancient eliminativism.

Once we are more familiar with the philosophical views and stages upon which Protagoras' Secret Doctrine is built, we can try to make good philosophical sense of it. This is done in chapter two, '*Twins and dharmas. Protagoras and Vasubandhu on a two-tier ontology of tropes*'. In this chapter Protagoras' Secret Doctrine is interpreted as a theory of tropes. In doing so, I challenge a recent interpretation by Christopher Buckels, who, while recognizing the plausibility of Protagoras' Secret Doctrine as a theory of tropes, maintains that it does not ultimately work because it fails to address the problem of fundamental/derivate tropes.

Chapter 3, '*Gorgias and Nāgārjuna on nihilism*', offers a comparative attempt to understand some of the arguments Gorgias and Nāgārjuna put forward in their works as nihilist arguments. In contrast with traditional scholarship that takes Gorgias' moves in *On What Is Not* as an exercise in rhetorical art, I provide a careful analysis of Gorgias' arguments that nothing is, claiming that they can be taken as aimed at ontological nihilism. This point is strengthened once it is realized that the nihilist arguments Gorgias puts forward have strikingly close analogies with a set of very similar nihilist arguments that Nāgārjuna offers in some of his works. While I stop short of claiming that both Gorgias and Nāgārjuna are nihilist philosophers tout court, I submit that a nihilist interpretation of their thought could help reassess the full meaning of their philosophies as well as showing us that there was a common nihilist trend in both Greek and Buddhist philosophies.

Chapter 4, 'On things. The origin and genealogy of Pyrrho's metaphysics', is about the genealogy and origin of Pyrrho's metaphysics. In this chapter I return to the Aristocles passage, to argue for a metaphysical reading of it; here it is shown that Pyrrho held a radical metaphysical thesis about things, that is, that they are undifferentiated, unstable and indeterminate. It is also shown that Pyrrho's radical views are not fully novel in ancient Greek philosophy, since a close parallelism between Pyrrho's indeterminacy thesis and Protagoras' Secret Doctrine is drawn. This parallelism does not exclude the fact that Pyrrho's views have also close analogies with similar doctrines held in early Buddhism. Instead of arguing for historical influence in way or another, in this chapter I claim that in his encounter with Indian philosophy Pyrrho is likely to have been the actual witness of a similarity of views between East and West.

The last two chapters deal with the Cyrenaics. In Chapter 5, 'The Cyrenaics on indeterminacy', I argue that metaphysical indeterminacy is a view that can consistently and coherently attributed to the Cyrenaics. Relying on my previous work in this area,[22] I challenge the traditional sceptical interpretation of the Cyrenaics, on the basis of which they, as sceptics, did not hold any metaphysical thesis about the material world. I examine much of the available evidence to show that it can be read as pointing towards indeterminacy. The main thesis this chapter argues for is that the kind of indeterminacy about material things the Cyrenaics may have been committed to is something very similar to the metaphysical positions about things held by Pyrrho and Protagoras. In this way, the elusiveness that material objects seem to display in the context of Cyrenaic philosophy cannot be explained in light of our epistemological deficiencies but on the assumption that things in the world are indeterminate ontologically.

The sixth chapter, 'The Cyrenaics on solipsism and privacy', deals with the problem of solipsism in the Cyrenaics. In Chapter 5 it is shown that the material world for the Cyrenaics is ontologically indeterminate and elusive. For the Cyrenaics on the other hand, we are always infallible aware of what we feel and perceive. In Cyrenaic thinking, the elusiveness of material objects is thus contrasted with the untransferable privacy of our affections. On the basis of this picture, one may thus wonder whether the subject is the only truly existing item for the Cyrenaics. In this chapter, I first assess the evidence on Cyrenaic solipsism to show why some views endorsed by the Cyrenaics appear to commit them to solipsism. I then deal with an underestimated argument on language attributed to the Cyrenaics, whose logic implies that after all the Cyrenaics cannot have endorsed a radical solipsism. Yet, by drawing an illuminating parallel with Wittgenstein's argument on private language and inner sensations, I make a case for the Cyrenaics to have subscribed to a sort of residual solipsism, which in turn helps us to understand the notion of Cyrenaic privacy to a fuller extent.

1

Protagoras' Secret Doctrine: An exercise in ancient eliminativism

We start off our journey into ancient kinds of eliminativism by looking in close detail at an incredibly philosophically rich section of one of Plato's most read dialogue, the *Theaetetus*. In that dialogue, which has attracted the attention of contemporary philosophers for ages, Socrates develops a lengthy discussion with the mathematicians Theaetetus and Theodorus of Cyrene. Under Socrates' guidance and Theodorus' support, the brilliant Theaetetus is questioned as to try to understand what knowledge actually is. In the context of the dialogue, Theaetetus comes up with three accounts of knowledge (in addition to an initial list of items that is quickly discharged by Socrates as inappropriate but that may help to find out actual instances of knowledge):[1] (1) knowledge as perception; (2) knowledge as true belief; (3) knowledge as true belief with an explanatory logos. All these definitions of knowledge are heavily scrutinized and, at the end, all rejected as being wrong, ill-suited or incomplete. Yet the arrays of philosophical arguments of deep sophistication that are presented throughout the discussion are such to impress each and every philosopher. Since the dialogue is so rich and philosophically intricate, the majority of the commentators or readers have focused on the main thread of the argument, often leaving aside some other minor sections that I think Plato constructed with the same sophistication and in-depth approach of the major ones.

Among these minor sections (with the understanding that 'minor' is here to be read as 'attracting less scholarly attention'), there is one that deals with Protagoras' Secret Doctrine. It is a section of the *Theaetetus* where very original philosophical views are introduced and discussed. It grows out from a preceding section where Protagoras' view that Man is the Measure of All things is debated. For the time being, let us focus on the key-features of Protagoras'

Secret Doctrine, since it represents an excellent philosophical introduction to the topic of ancient eliminativism, which we shall be dealing with in this book.

Protagoras' relativism and the Secret Doctrine

In the *Theaetetus* we find the first important affirmation of relativism in the history of Western thought. Theaetetus' initial definition that knowledge is perception is immediately equated by Socrates with Protagoras' doctrine that Man is the Measure of All Things: 'Man is the measure of all things, of the things that are, that they are, and of the things that are not, that they are not' (*Tht.* 152a3–5).[2] Protagoras' Maxim, which is said to have been the opening statement of Protagoras' *Truth*, has so far received many alternative readings.[3] Plato's Socrates gives his own interpretation of it at the very beginning of the first section of the *Theaetetus* (151e–186a), namely the section where Theaetetus' first definition of knowledge as perception is put under intense scrutiny. According to Socrates, with his almost oracular wording Protagoras' Maxim alludes to a form of relativism that is mainly perceptual but that also has an ontological commitment. In Socrates' opinion, with his maxim that Man is the Measure of All Things Protagoras aims to suggest that all perceptions are legitimate, in so far as they are all relative to the single percipient. If two people feel a blowing wind and one of them feels it as cold and the other as not cold, Protagoras will be happy to say that 'the wind is cold for the person who is shivering, and not for the person who isn't' (*Tht.* 152b8–9). If each thing is as each of us perceives it to be, all perceptions will be true for each of us, individually taken.

Among the conflicting appearances arising when different people perceive an object, there is no perception that is uniquely correct, against all the others being mistaken: for Protagoras each perception is true because each perception is relative to a perceiver. It cannot be otherwise, since there is no reality out there independently of how we perceive it. This being the case, Theaetetus' definition that knowledge is perception is indeed true for Protagoras. As Socrates sums up: 'A thing's appearing to someone, then, is the same as his perceiving it, in the case of hot things and of everything like that. For how each of us perceives a thing is likely also to be how it is for each of us'

(*Tht.* 152c1–3); 'as befits knowledge, then, perception is always of what is, and never plays us false' (c5–6).

I am not concerned here whether the way Socrates takes Protagoras' Maxim in the *Theaetetus* is the actual way in which Protagoras intended his Maxim to be taken (myself thinking that in dealing with Protagoras, despite some inevitable intrusions on his part, Plato displays a quite respectable level of historical accuracy).[4] Whether he is trustworthy or not as a Protagorean exegete, Plato's Socrates is in any case well aware that his reading of Protagoras' Maxim as a form of relativism raises a vast array of philosophical questions that soon need to be addressed, since his very first handling of Protagoras' relativism, while being illuminating, leaves out more than what it actually reveals.

Socrates remarks that, in order to get its full meaning, Protagoras' relativism is to be read in conjunction with a Secret Doctrine of his, more literally a doctrine that Protagoras 'revealed to his disciples in secret'.[5] As we have briefly seen, Socrates' reading of Protagoras Maxim provides us with a form of relativism that closely links perceptions to ontology, that is, to the actual way material things are supposed to be. Ontological concerns are central in Protagoras' Secret Doctrine too, this doctrine being initially built upon two interrelated views, one metaphysical, and the other semantic:

> I will tell you a theory that certainly ought not to be written off. It's to the effect that actually nothing is just one thing, itself by itself, and that you cannot refer to a thing correctly by any description whatever. If you call something big, it will appear as small as well, and if you call it heavy, it will appear as light too; and similarly with everything, just because – so the theory says – nothing is one, whether a one something or a one any sort of thing. (*Tht.* 152d2–8)

The metaphysical view at the kernel of Protagoras' Secret Doctrine is that nothing is just one thing, itself by itself. That is, 'nothing is one, whether a one something or one any sort of thing'. These are actually two distinct metaphysical views, closely interrelated but also distinct views. The first, stronger view is that no material item is one determinate thing. I shall label this view as 'strong indeterminacy': things in the material world are ontologically indeterminate, in so far as no material item is one determinate thing. The second, milder metaphysical view central to Protagoras' Secret Doctrine is that no material item is attributed a determinate secondary quality. I shall label this view as 'mild indeterminacy', since it attaches indeterminacy to specific properties of material items, not to things in themselves. Mild indeterminacy simply prescribes that no one thing is determinately one way or the other: the wind in Socrates' example is in itself neither cold nor hot (at 152b4–5). On the other hand, strong indeterminacy proposes a rather challenging, more radical view: nothing is one determinate thing in itself. Obviously enough, if the existence-predicate is understood as a standard predicate, from mild indeterminacy we shall easily get strong indeterminacy; in detailing the metaphysical core of Protagoras' Secret Doctrine, however, Socrates often conflates strong and mild indeterminacy.[6]

In addition to these quite original metaphysical views, Protagoras' Secret doctrine contains a semantic view, which, as I take it, grows out – and builds upon – the metaphysical views just illustrated: if nothing is one thing or is determinately qualified in one way or the other, you cannot refer to such a thing correctly by any description whatsoever. As Socrates says: 'If you call something big, it will appear as small as well, and if you call it heavy, it will appear as light too; and similarly with everything'. As far as the semantic thesis is concerned, the emphasis in Socrates' words is put at first on the actual linkage between semantic interchangeability and mild indeterminacy: that is, what is going to be termed as 'large' now will be attributed the property of smallness at a later stage and, hence, will be called as 'small' by then. On the other hand, it will be soon obvious that Plato intends semantic ineffability to be applied to thing in themselves too, not only to properties of things.[7] Proper names will not be able to name the very thing that naturally they are supposed to name. What is going to be threatened, in the very context of Protagoras' Secret Doctrine is the semantic linkage between a thing and its proper name, that is, the very same linkage that ultimately provides meaningfulness to the words we use.[8]

The two metaphysical views about indeterminacy and the related semantic view of ineffability would already constitute a quite original family of doctrines, but Plato is not fully satisfied and adds a fourth important element in Protagoras' Secret Doctrine, namely flux. On the basis of the story Socrates tells Theaetetus, the metaphysical view and its semantic counterpart have a deeper origin in the theory of flux: nothing is one thing and cannot properly be referred to with any description whatsoever *because*

> All things are in the process of coming to be through motion, and change in general, and mixture with each other; nothing ever is, it's always coming to be. (*Tht.* 152d8–e1)

As far as I can see, then, Protagoras' Secret Doctrine is a quite elaborated theory. Its core are two interrelated metaphysical theses about indeterminacy, which have a semantic consequence: the ineffability of things and of the properties we usually attach to things. The origin of indeterminacy is flux. Things cannot be determinate entities and cannot have determinate properties because everything is in flux. Nothing is because everything is coming to be.

A new theory of perception: Stage One (*Tht.* 153d8–154b9)

In dealing with Protagoras' Secret Doctrine, we are thus confronted with a rather original mix of philosophical views. What sort of philosophical gain is one expected to get when Protagoras' initial profession of relativism is conjoined with his Secret Doctrine? We have seen that Protagoras' relativism, as Socrates interprets it, is mainly an epistemological thesis that also has a quite clear ontological commitment: things are as we perceive them to be. In Protagoras' view, there is no real wind, but a family of blowing winds relative to each perceiver. On the other hand, Protagoras' Secret Doctrine is made up by metaphysical and semantic views, while it lacks, at least *prima facie*, any epistemological concern. What is, after all, the epistemological gain for Protagoras' relativism when his Secret Doctrine is brought into the picture?

In order to help answer the question, Socrates is keen to offer Theaetetus a further explanation aimed to show how Protagoras' relativistic epistemology is actually enriched by the contribution of his Secret Doctrine. Socrates splits this explanation in two parts, one preliminary at *Tht.* 153d8–154b9, the other more informative at *Tht.* 156a3–157c5 (when the doctrine of the subtler thinkers makes its appearance). Let us label these two parts of Socrates' further explanation as, respectively, 'Stage One' and 'Stage Two' explanation.

In Stage One, Socrates shows Theaetetus how to locate Protagoras' Secret Doctrine in the context of Protagorean relativism. He does so by detailing the first rudiments of a quite peculiar theory of perception:

> Socrates: The best way to think of that theory [sc. The Secret Doctrine], my friend, is this. In the case of the eyes, first of all, you shouldn't think of what you call white colour as some other thing outside your eyes, or within the eyes, and neither should you assign it some particular location; if you do, it will surely then be fixed and resting, and come to be no longer in the process of coming to be. (*Tht.* 153d8–e-3)

> Let us follow out what we were saying just now, and posit nothing that is just one thing, itself by itself. That way we'll find that black or white or any colour you like must have been generated from the eyes' meeting the relevant motion, and that we actually call colour in each case won't be either what is doing the striking or what is being struck, but rather something that has come to be in between the two, peculiar to each. Or would you prefer to insist that as each colour appears to you, so it appears to a dog or whatever other living creature too? (*Tht.* 153e4–154a4)

> What about another human being? Does the way anything appears to someone else match the way it appears to you? Are you sure about that? Aren't you much surer that it won't appear the same to you because you yourself won't ever be the same as yourself? (*Tht.* 154a6–9)

Protagoras' relativism appears to get a new meaning when it is interpreted under the constraints of Protagoras' Secret Doctrine. We have seen that the core metaphysical view of the Secret Doctrine is that nothing is one thing, itself by itself. On the basis of Socrates' own words, I have given two different versions of this view: either no material item is one determinate thing (strong indeterminacy) or no material item is attributed a determinate secondary property (mild indeterminacy).

Both versions of indeterminacy are well present in the development of the theory of perception Socrates illustrates Theaetetus at Stage One. As for mild indeterminacy, no material item is attributed a determinate property, such as a colour, because, in the actual context of the perceptual theory Socrates is developing out of the Secret Doctrine, any given colour is understood as the result of the eyes meeting the relevant motion of perception. More precisely, in the world of perennial flux that is the ultimate *rasion d'etre* of Protagoras' Secret Doctrine, the perceived colour is to be taken as the result of the process of interaction between what is being struck on the one hand and what does the striking on the other. This being the case, each colour becomes relative to a single act of perceiving and, consequently, relative to a sole and unique percipient. Only when it is correctly linked with the main metaphysical views illustrated in the Secret Doctrine, Protagoras' relativism is given a wider application and, consequently, a stronger philosophical appeal. It is only in the context of the Secret Doctrine that Protagoras' relativism will show its full potential by sketching a quite peculiar theory of relative perception. For Protagoras, perceptions are relative to the single percipient exactly because the individual percipient, at the very moment when perception takes place, gets involved with the perceived object. In the temporary contact between what is being perceived and who does the perceiving, perception arises as something peculiar to each of them, that is, to the individual percipient as well as to the perceived object.[9]

Perception is thus relative in so far as it provides a temporary epistemological linkage between the two poles interacting in the perceptual process, namely the perceived object on the one hand, and the individual percipient on the other. Although Socrates' wider understanding of Protagoras' relativism offers us a quite peculiar theory of perception, the story is not yet complete because strong indeterminacy is now fully back in the picture: the two poles of the perceptual processes are no one thing in themselves. Socrates asks Theaetetus:

> What about another human being? Does the way anything appears to someone else match the way it appears to you? Are you sure about that? Aren't you much surer that it won't appear the same to you because you yourself won't ever be the same as yourself? (*Tht.* 154a6–9)

On the ground of strong indeterminacy, the individual percipient is thus no one thing, ontologically stable and determinate. His identity keeps changing over time. This is a further reason that makes Protagoras' relativism even more radical: since the individual percipient is not the same person over time, the way things appear to him are not only relative to him but also relative to him *at the very moment when perception takes place*. What appears white to him now may appear grey to him within an hour because within an hour he will not be the same person he is now.

A new theory of perception: Stage Two (the Subtler Thinkers: *Tht.* 156a–157c)

By means of Socrates' midwifery, we have learned that, in order to be fully appreciated, Protagoras' relativism is to be read in conjunction with his Secret Doctrine. We have also learned how Protagoras' relativism is to be developed into a peculiar theory of perception to show its full philosophical implications. Socrates has illustrated the new interpretation of Protagoras' relativism in one preliminary stage, that is, at Stage One. There are, however, other aspects to be clarified, and other questions to be asked, as far as Protagorean theories are concerned. What has happened to the semantic aspect of Protagoras' Secret Doctrine? There is no mention of it in Socrates' Stage One explanation. At the same time, while it tells us very clearly the metaphysical status of perceiving subjects, as well as showing how perceptions arise in the perceptual process, Socrates' Stage One explanation does not spell out the metaphysical status of material things in that very process. We have just seen that the perceiving subject is not one determinate thing: what about perceived objects? Are they ontologically unstable/indeterminate as well? If so, how unstable/indeterminate are they?

In order to clarify these important aspects of Protagoras' theories, Socrates gives us what I have labelled a Stage Two explanation. Socrates provides the second, wider explanation at *Tht.* 156a3–157c5, where he illustrates a theory of perception whose paternity is to be attributed to some subtler thinkers.[10] For our own purposes in the present chapter the question of the identity of the subtler thinkers is not important. The natural way to take the theory of perception of the subtler thinkers is to understand it as a more elaborate version of the theory of perception that Socrates has already illustrated at *Tht.* 153d8–154a9, that is, at Stage One. If this is the case, the more refined – perhaps the 'subtler' (to use Plato's own word) – theory of perception we are just about to read will be understood as a further development of Protagoras' relativism. What does the more refined version of the subtler thinkers' theory of perception add to Protagoras' theory of perception as this is illustrated at *Tht.* 153d8–154a9? In other words, how is Stage Two related to Stage One? Does the new, more refined version fill in the philosophical gaps already noted, as well as answering the questions we have been asking about the ontological status of perceived objects?

When he illustrates the first details of the theory of perception of the subtler thinkers, Socrates makes clear that the new version of the theory strictly adheres to the idea that 'everything is change and there is nothing beside change' (*Tht.* 156a5); he also remarks that the new version of the theory is, as it was in the case of the Secret Doctrine, a doctrine for initiated people. As soon as he has highlighted the centrality of flux and change in the theory of the subtler thinkers, Socrates immediately says that there are two forms of change, each one with different capacities:

> Of change there were two forms, each unlimited in plurality but with different powers, one to act, the other to be acted upon. From the coming together of these two motions, and the friction of one against the other, offspring come into being – unlimited number of them, but twins in every case, one twin being what is perceived, the other a perception, emerging simultaneously with what is perceived and being generated along with it. Well, for the perceptions we possess names such a seeing, hearing, smelling, cooling down, or burning up, ones we call pleasures and pains, too, desires and fears, and others besides – an unlimited number that lack names as well as a huge range that are named. (*Tht.* 156a6–b7)

The key aspect of the subtler thinkers' theory of perception is that, everything being in flux, there are two kinds of motion, unlimited in numbers, with opposite powers. From the coming together and the friction of these two motions with opposite powers, offspring comes into being as twins: on the one hand, there is the perception, on the other what is being perceived.

After this, Socrates is immediately keen to show the conceptual relationship between the new, more refined version of the theory of perception and the less sophisticated version of it, namely the one developed briefly at Stage One.[11] In addition to specifying that motions can be quick and slow, Socrates offers the following picture as evidence as to how the perceptual process actually takes place in the world of the subtler thinkers:

> So when something commensurate with an eye has come into the neighbourhood of an eye, together the eye and it generate both whiteness

and a perception twinned with whiteness – two things that would never come to be if either the eye or the other thing has approached anything else. Sight then moves between them from the eyes, whiteness from the co-producer of the colour, and now – hey presto – the eye is full of sight; now it sees, having become, certainly not sight, rather a seeing eye, and what has co-generated the colour has been filled full of whiteness, having become for its part not whiteness but white, whether a white piece of wood or a white stone or whatever thing happened to have become coloured with this sort of colour. (*Tht.* 156d3–e8)

This is a striking account of perception, and one that is perfectly able to explain how the twin-offspring comes into proper birth: perception (of white in the example Socrates makes) is seen as arising from the temporary and accidental encounter between the proper sense-organ (the seeing eye) and the perceived 'object' (although the term 'object' shouldn't be used, as we will see shortly), which appears to be white on the occasion. It is worth noting that in such a picture of the perceptual process, there is no explicit reference to the role of the perceiving subject, which is reduced to his sense-organs (while in the less sophisticated version of the theory of perception illustrated at Stage One the emphasis was indeed on the subject performing the perceptual activity).

Socrates makes the example of visual perception but he remarks that what he has just said applies to all kinds of perceptions, because 'nothing is, itself by itself, as we were saying before; rather, it is in coming together with each other that all things and all sorts of things come to be, from their changing' (*Tht.* 157a1–3). The picture is made even more radical by the fact that

> it is not possible to get a stable fix, in the one case, even on which of them is doing the acting and which is being acted upon, for neither is there anything acting before it comes together with what is acted on, nor anything being acted on before it comes together with what is acting; and what does the acting when together with one thing turns out to be what is acted on when together with something else. (*Tht.* 157a3–9)

The main features of the theory of perception of the subtler thinkers confirm why it should be seen as a more sophisticated development of the theory of perception illustrated by Socrates at Stage One: movement and change are now understood as having two different powers. Perception on the one hand, and what is perceived on the other are to be seen as twins originating from the temporary encounter of two elements that are in perennial process of changing and that are on some occasions acted on, on others acting on.

As a way of conclusion Socrates stresses the conceptual linkage between the theory of perception of the subtler thinkers and Protagoras' Secret Doctrine:

> The consequence of all this, according to the theory, is that nothing – as we were saying at the beginning – is just one thing, itself by itself, but instead is always coming to be in relation to something. The verb 'is' must be removed from every context, even though we ourselves have been forced to use it many times over even just now, out of habit and lack of knowledge. In fact, according to these wise people's theory, we shouldn't consent to using 'something', or 'somebody's', or 'mine', or 'this', or 'that', or any other name that brings things to a standstill. Instead our utterances should conform to nature and have things 'coming to be', 'being made', 'passing away', and 'altering' (…). The rule applies to talk about the individual case and about many collected together, the sort of collection for which people posit entities like human being, and rock, and so on with each living creature and form. (*Tht.* 157a9–c2)

Earlier we have seen that the explanation Socrates gives at Stage One (to show how Protagoras' relativism is to be understood properly only when taken together with his Secret Doctrine) was in need of further specifications. Socrates' Stage Two explanation, namely the theory of perception developed by the subtler thinkers at *Tht.* 156a3ff., provides us with important clarifications about movement, change and perceptual processes. It also tells us more about the two points left behind in Stage One explanation, that is, the ontological status of perceived objects and the problem of semantic ineffability. By reading Socrates' Stage Two explanation, we are now aware that not only perceiving subjects but also objects of perceptions are ontologically indeterminate. Their identity is ontologically unstable, since everything keeps flowing and changing all the time and in all respects. Indeed, and strictly speaking, there are neither actual objects nor real subjects in the perceptual process. As Socrates remarks, there are no rocks and no human being there. Because of the absence of ontological determinacy, we are caught in the trap of semantic ineffability: we cannot name material things because there is, properly speaking, nothing there to be named. The referential linkage between a thing and its proper name is broken, because there is no proper thing there to be named. Our language should be fully replaced by another language, more capable to capture the fluidity of matter.

The Secret Doctrine and the New Theory of Perception: Viable theories?

Protagoras' relativism has travelled much, from its very first appearance in the dialogue at *Tht.* 152a to its final re-interpretation at *Tht.* 156a–157c (Stage Two explanation) via the intermediate steps of the Secret Doctrine and Socrates' Stage One explanation. The actual combination of Protagoras' relativism with his Secret Doctrine has produced a quite peculiar theory of perception, which Socrates illustrates in two stages. The four philosophical views that are at the core of Protagoras' Secret Doctrine are fully present in the theory of perception Socrates illustrates at Stage Two. The four views dealt with in the Secret Doctrine section, it may be worth repeating, are the following ones: (1) nothing has one determinate property (mild indeterminacy); (2) nothing is one thing, itself by itself (strong indeterminacy); (3) semantic ineffability: you cannot refer to a thing correctly by any description; (4) everything is in flux.

In the theory of perception illustrated at Stage Two, we find the following claims: (1) nothing has one determinate property: the property of 'whiteness' does not belong permanently and determinately to a rock now appearing white to me because the rock appearing white to me now as well as my perception of white are the twin-birth of a process soon to be terminated. (2) Nothing is one thing in itself by itself: either what is being perceived and who does the perceiving are not, strictly speaking, material items with an enduring identity over time. There are no material items in the world, since everything is a motion and everything is in motion. What we perceive as stable material items such as rocks and human beings are simply motions or collection with a slightly longer durability. (3) The world being deprived of material items with an enduring stability over time, and everything being in perennial flux, we can't use proper names to name things in the world, since there are no things to be named. (4) The world is thus a world of processes and interactions, a world of motion, changing and flux with no residual ontological stability.

It is in only this picture that Protagoras' relativism gets its full significance. Since everything is in flux and is motion; since there are no proper material items in the world apart from processes and interactions, perception can only be seen as the temporary product of the causal encounter between the sense-organs and what is being perceived. If this is the case, perception will only be relative to the subject carrying out the perceptual activity, at the very moment when perception takes place.

Together with the initial definition of knowledge as perception (*Tht.* 151e4–6) and with Heraclitus' flux-theory, Protagoras' relativism is part of Theaetetus' first child, that is, part of the first sustained effort Theaetetus makes to understand what knowledge is.[12] A common way (labelled as Reading B by Myles Burnyeat in *The Theaetetus of Plato*, 1990)[13] to read the first section of the *Theaetetus* is to take it as a *reductio ad absurdum*: the thesis that knowledge is perception (KP) entails Protagoras' relativism (R), which, in turn, entails Heraclitus' theory of flux (H), which is ultimately unacceptable because it makes language impossible. While Reading B has surely some exegetical strength, I don't think it is a fair way to understand the overall logic of *Theaetetus* 151e–186a. In dealing with the three main views that are at the core of the first part of Plato's *Theaetetus* (namely KP, R and H), Plato is confronted with other doctrines that arise, or are conceptually closely linked, with the three main ones on stage. That is, while dealing with Protagoras' relativism, we have been confronted with Protagoras' Secret Doctrine, which itself is built upon four relevant views, only one of which (namely H) is going to receive a fuller treatment by Plato later in the dialogue.

In *Theaetetus* 151e–186a, Plato offers three main types of refutation: of Protagoras' relativism (at *Tht.* 170–171, with a further refutation at *Tht.* 177c5–179b of a modified version of Protagoras' relativism as this is further developed at *Tht.* 166a–168c5); of the thesis that knowledge is perception (at *Tht.* 184b–186e); of Heraclitus' flux-theory (at *Tht.* 181c–183c). That is, in the first section of the *Theaetetus* Plato provides important attempts to refute the three main philosophical theses that are being discussed at *Tht.* 151e–186a: KP, R and H. Nowhere in the *Theaetetus* will one find Plato trying to argue directly against some corollary views, such as Protagoras' Secret Doctrine, which in the economy of the dialogue is seen as arising from the thread of the main philosophical discussion brought forward by

Socrates, Theaetetus and the mathematician from Cyrene, Theodorus. More in particular, one of the three main theses under scrutiny in the first part of the dialogue (that is, H) is going to be tentatively refuted by Plato at *Tht.* 181c–183c but not in itself but because, according to Plato, its adoption will ultimately lead to the impossibility of language.[14]

In the *Theaetetus* there is therefore no refutation, either direct or indirect, of Protagoras' Secret Doctrine and of the main views around which it is built; in addition, there is no refutation too of the theory of perception that is the main outcome of Protagoras' relativism and his Secret Doctrine. Yet the Secret Doctrine section, with its two philosophical appendices (Stage One and Stage Two theories), is generally admired for its appeal but easily discharged because it is usually regarded as philosophically untenable. The views around which it is built, however, are not absurd views to defend nowadays, as we have learned in the Introduction. The very idea that material items can be eliminated, in different ways and for different reasons, from the ontological apparatus of the world is something that has some currency in contemporary debates. One of the main claims of this book is that different kinds of eliminativism were already well present in Ancient Greek philosophy and that eliminativism was a vitally relevant view in ancient metaphysics. We may have been so far unable to locate it and include it into a convincing account of ancient metaphysics for lack of interest and/or philosophical myopia. For a variety of reasons, we are now in a much better position to assess the richness of ancient metaphysical debates by including eliminativism into the picture.

We have started our journey by looking in detail at the Secret Doctrine section of Plato's *Theaetetus* because in this way we have been shown what I think is the best introduction to the main tenets of ancient eliminativism. There is also a second reason for choosing the Secret Doctrine as the best introduction to ancient eliminativism, a second reason that is strictly connected to the first one. All the main Greek thinkers that are the protagonists of this book have been linked to the Secret Doctrine section of the *Theaetetus*. Obviously enough, Protagoras is the main figure here, since Socrates claims that the Secret Doctrine is what he taught to his pupils in secret. But also the Cyrenaics have been connected to the Secret Doctrine, for some scholars have thought they are the subtler thinkers Socrates mentions at *Tht.* 156a3 and whose theories are best explained in Stage Two.[15] Democritus and the atomists have been called into the picture more recently, because the theories expounded in the Secret Doctrine section are seen as arising from/compatible with an atomistic conception of the world.[16] Lastly, Richard Bett has suggested that Pyrrho's views on metaphysical indeterminacy find an illuminating parallel with the views around which the Secret Doctrine is centred.[17] Moreover, the doctrines discussed in the Secret Doctrine provide a striking analogy with some main metaphysical doctrines of Buddhism, as I shall show in Chapter 4.

The Secret Doctrine is therefore a crucial piece of evidence for ancient eliminativism. My view on the Secret Doctrine is that Plato is making it up on the basis of historical evidence. That is, it is as if Plato detected a common metaphysical approach (also resulting into an original perceptual doctrine) among a variety of philosophical views (most probably, those held at his time by Protagoras, the Cyrenaics and the early atomists). This common metaphysical approach is what I have labelled 'eliminativism'. Plato is thus our early, important and detailed source for a view that was much more widespread in ancient philosophy than we could have thought at first sight.

2

Twins and dharmas. Protagoras and Vasubandhu on a two-tier ontology of tropes

In the previous chapter, we have gone through the main features of Protagoras' Secret Doctrine, from indeterminacy to flux and ineffability, via the reconstruction in two stages of a complex theory of perception that has both epistemological and metaphysical implications. For this book's purposes, we will now focus on the metaphysical issues at the heart of Protagoras' Secret Doctrine. In the previous chapter, the main ontological features of that doctrine have already been highlighted. From the fact that in the context of Protagoras' Secret Doctrine nothing is one thing in itself or has any properties on its own, we have seen that material items such as stones and human being are best understood as not existent as determinate items with ontological durability over time.[1]

What we are going to do now is to see how we can make good sense, philosophically, of this peculiar view about material objects as this is sketched in the Secret Doctrine. While doing so, we shall be confronted with recent work on the ontology of Protagoras' Secret Doctrine (such as Buckels 2016). At the same time, to offer an interpretation of the Secret Doctrine that is both coherent and appealing, we will look for inspiration in the theory of dharmas developed by the Buddhist philosopher Vasubandhu, which in fact, has striking similarities with the sort of metaphysical outlook that we see as operating in Protagoras' Secret Doctrine.[2]

Stage Two theory of perception

Given that plenty of details about Protagoras' Secret Doctrine have been provided in the previous chapter, we shall be now concentrating on its last development, that is, Stage Two theory of perception. Remember that in both Stage One and Stage Two theories of perception, the emphasis is put on everything being (in) flux. Let me quote once again the opening of this Stage Two theory:

> (A) Of motion there were two forms, each unlimited in plurality but with different powers, one to act, the other to be acted upon. From the coming together of these two motions, and the friction of one against the other, offspring come into being – unlimited number of them, but twins in every case, one twin being what is perceived, the other a perception, emerging simultaneously with what is perceived and being generated along with it. Well, for the perceptions we possess names such a seeing, hearing, smelling, cooling down, or burning up, ones we call pleasures and pains, too, desires and fears, and others besides – an unlimited number that lack names as well as a huge range that are named. (*Tht.* 156a6–b7)

We have thus two different kinds of motion, each unlimited in number, one with an active power, the other with a passive power. Remember also that the active power may become passive on another occasion.[3] It is from the friction and coming together of these two kinds of motion that perceptual/ontological twins are produced: on the one hand, there is what is (being) perceived in the context of that temporary encounter between the two motions, on the other hand, there is the perception. Socrates provides more illuminating details on this process:

> (B) So when something commensurate with an eye has come into the neighbourhood of an eye, together the eye and it generate both whiteness and a perception twinned with whiteness – two things that would never come to be if either the eye or the other thing has approached anything else. Sight then moves between them from the eyes, whiteness from the co-producer of the colour, and now – hey presto – the eye is full of sight; now it sees, having become, certainly not sight, rather a seeing eye, and what has co-generated the colour has been filled full of whiteness, having become for its part not whiteness but white, whether a white piece of wood or a white stone or whatever thing happened to have become coloured with this sort of colour. (*Tht.* 156d3–e8)

More sophisticated twin-products of the temporary encounter of double-powered motions are now born: on the one hand, there is whiteness, and on the other, the perception twinned with it. If we look closer at the process, we understand that there is a *particular seeing eye*, not a sight, which sees a *particular 'thing'*, that is, a white stone at that very time. After a moment, that seeing eye and that white stone are something else, another 'seeing eye' and another 'stone', perhaps black on the occasion of a new encounter.

This theory of perception is highly original and philosophically captivating. But what are we talking about here? In the context of Protagoras' Secret Doctrine, can we really talk of objects and subjects in the perceptual process and, at large, in the ontological apparatus of the material world out there? Previously I have commented that on the basis of Stage Two theory of perception, we may well assume that there are neither actual objects nor real subjects, since every material item in the world of Protagoras is ontologically indeterminate.[4] So, if there are neither objects nor subjects, what will be left with? The usual answer is 'processes', but more precisely processes of what? It does seem that to interpret the metaphysics of Protagoras' Secret Doctrine as an ontology of processes is a too simplistic account of what is really at issue in one of the most fascinating sections in the whole Platonic corpus. Processes are indeed a central element in the Secret Doctrine, but this fact does not tell us anything about the ontological status of material objects in the world of Protagoras as this is depicted by Plato in this part of the *Theaetetus*. Are material objects in the Secret Doctrine completely replaced by processes? Or are there any possibilities that, while being the essentially dominant element in the ontology of the Secret Doctrine, processes allow for a metaphysics of flux where material objects still play a marginal role, yet one that still needs to be worked out?

Slow and swift motions

To try answering these questions, we are going to dig deeper into Protagoras' Secret Doctrine by taking into full account another feature of it that has not been mentioned in the previous chapter, that is, the speed of motions in the Stage Two theory of perception. The diverse speed of motions plays an important role in the Stage Two theory of perception and helps us answer those questions about the ontological status of material objects we are now asking.

As seen, Socrates tells Theaetetus that in the Stage Two theory of perceptions, there are two kinds of motions, either with active or passive power. This is also interchangeable, so that an active power later becomes passive and vice versa. It is through the encounter and friction of these two kinds of motions that a twin-ontology is produced, with an offspring of pairing perceptions and perceived 'things' arising temporarily and at the same time, out of evanescing processes. Socrates now gives us new information on motions. He says:

> (C) All these things are in motion, just as we say (see passage A above); and their motion is distinguished by its swiftness or slowness. What is slow has its motion in one and the same place, and in relation to the things in the immediate neighbourhood; in this way it generates () and the offspring are swifter, as they move through space, and their motion takes the form of spatial movement (passage B follows). (*Tht.* 156c7–d2)

With motions not only being active and passive but also swift and slow, we have now a more definitive picture of the perceptual process in the Stage Two theory of perception. We have now a fourfold categorization of motions into active, passive, swift and slow. Considering these four categories of motions, here is a picture of the full perceptual process as sketched by Burnyeat in his *Commentary*:[5]

Table 1 Adaption from Burnyeat 1990

Slow passive	Quick	Quick	Slow active
Eye	Sight	Whiteness	Stone

According to this picture, in the perceptual process where the four different motions take place, the slow active motion (what we traditionally conceive of as a 'stone') meets the slow passive motion (what we may call 'the seeing eye'); from this brief encounter, an offspring of swift motions generates. These swift motions are always twins: on the one hand we have the generated whiteness, more precisely the white stone, and on the other the seeming eye full of sight (of whiteness). In the perceptual process as this is sketched in the Stage Two theory, everything is then motion and in motion: the slower motions seem to be provided with more temporal as well as ontological durability so that they can somehow generate the swifter motions, which are – as such – extremely quick and evanescing. The perception of whiteness and the seeing eye full of sight last very little (namely the very time of their short-lived generation) and are immediately replaced by other twins, again produced by slower motions and again doomed to live a very short life. As we have noted above and as many commentators highlight, in this last development of Protagoras Secret Doctrine, material objects (such as things and people) become ontologically redundant.

Causal theory and phenomenalist interpretations

In the scholarship, there are two main ways to read the sophisticated theory of perception that is at the heart of Protagoras' Secret Doctrine: 'physical' versus 'metaphysical', to use Burnyeat's labels; 'Phenomenalist' and 'Causal Theory' Interpretations, to use Buckels' labels.[6] As for the Physical/Phenomenalist reading, in the ontology of motions that has provided us with the last development of Protagoras' Secret Doctrine, slow motions cannot cause swifter motions to exist, because slow motions cannot be material objects (whose existence is openly denied by the Secret Doctrine). The proposers of this interpretation reject any ontological (that is, 'causal') dependence of swift motions on slower motions, arguing that everything is a chain of motions, closely interconnected. As Day puts it: 'The slow fluxes are identified with the "aggregates", and thus are taken as being logically dependent on the "quicker" fluxes, as opposed to causing them.'[7] On his part, David Sedley writes that everything (that is, both slow and swift motions) are 'simply bundles of perceptual twins'.[8]

In this way, the phenomenalist interpretation makes the Secret Doctrine an ontology of property-particulars that arise out of temporary processes, with no material cause for their existence that is not wholly reducible to those processes. The phenomenalist interpretation in the end offers a plausible ontology for Protagoras' Secret Doctrine, but it does so by bypassing, or ignoring, a textual element that is indeed there for us to appreciate. Socrates openly says that swifter motions are produced by slower motions, namely the stone and the seeing eye (*Tht.* 156d3–e7). The property-particular ontology sketched by the Phenomenalist interpretation has not, so far, accounted for this two-tier ontology of slow/swift motions, with the former producing in some way the latter. Exactly because it ignores the fact that the text does make slow motions ontologically more fundamental than swift ones, the Phenomenalist interpretation has been challenged by the Causal Theory interpretation.

Against the Phenomenalist interpretation, the Casual Theory interpretation in fact argues for swift motions being generated by slower ones. In the context of the Causal Theory interpretation, slow motions are physical objects that are responsible, via causation, for the production of sensibles, that is, swifter motions. The Causal Theory interpretation too runs into some difficulties: while it takes into due account the ontological fundamentality of slow motions over swift ones, it however introduces a concept, that of material object, which is not ontologically admissible in the context of the Secret Doctrine. After all, if both the stone and the seeing eye are slow motions, well, they are traditional physical objects as we usually conceive of them. At the same time, while the Phenomenalist interpretation does not recognize a fundamental ontological distinction between slow and swift motions, the Causal Theory interpretation does introduce a distinction that is not in the text, that is, the one between physical objects (that is, material objects) and sensible objects (that is, objects of perception).

The revised version of the Causal Theory interpretation

Both the Phenomenalist and the Causal Theory interpretations are thus unsatisfactory as possible explanations of the ontology of Protagoras' Secret Doctrine. It is exactly because of this that an ingenious recent attempt by Christopher Buckles is aimed to solve these exegetical problems by offering a modified Causal Theory interpretation that, according to him, makes good sense of the ontology of the Secret Doctrine. In his interpretation, Buckles highlights that in the Secret Doctrine, we are given other information on material objects, since both human beings and stones are labelled as 'aggregates' (157b8–c1). Plato does not give further details on the nature of these aggregates but it is clear from the text that material objects such as stones are best seen as aggregates of sensibles (such as *this* whiteness, *that* hardness and so on) and human beings as aggregates of perceptions. (I note here that this characterization of aggregates fits well too with the Phenomenalist interpretation – this is a point that will receive due attention later in the chapter.) Such a description of material objects as aggregates is hardly reconcilable with the idea of physical objects (*qua* traditional objects) as slow motions that plays a fundamental role in the Causal Theory interpretation. For this reason, Buckles suggests that there is no need for someone endorsing a Causal reading of Protagoras' Secret Doctrine to endorse the idea that slow motions are physical objects generating swifter motions.

He suggests taking slow motions not as proper physical objects but as aggregates of powers, the other two-way feature of motions in Protagoras' Secret Doctrine (that is, active and passive powers: see above, passage A). In this way, once physical objects are replaced by aggregates, Buckles claims that the old problem for the Causal Theory interpretation is solved. No physical object plays a role in the ontological process of Protagoras' Secret Doctrine and everything is indeed (in) motion. As he writes: 'The original formulation of CTI (that is, the Causal Theory interpretation) was correct, then, but phrased misleadingly. There are swift motions which we subjectively aggregate and call sensible objects, but there are, objectively, not such objects. Those sensibles are produced by slow motions, which should not be called physical objects, since they are not physical and they are not objects. We should preserve Socrates' name for them – slow motions – or perhaps dub them powers; but physical objects will not do'.[9]

A problem with the revised version of the Causal Theory interpretation

After having provided his revised version of the Casual Theory interpretation, Buckles gives a brief, yet meaningful review of his overall interpretation of the ontology of the Secret Doctrine. He says: 'Sensibles particulars are bundles of sensibles, for example whiteness, hardness, loudness, etc. These sensibles can be understood as the tropes of contemporary metaphysics; they are particular instances of sensory properties, not universals (…). The bundling of tropes is not objective but subjective: man is the measure of what is, since each person bundles sensory properties into private objects. There are no objective objects: sensible particulars are subjective bundles of sensibles that exist only in relation to a (similarly bundled) perceiver'.[10] Again, as in the case of the Phenomenalist interpretation, even in Buckles' revised version of Causal Theory interpretation, the ontology of the Secret Doctrine is, ultimately, one of tropes, but with a further ontological distinction that on behalf of the Causal Theory interpretation Buckles makes: there are not only sensible particulars at work in the Secret Doctrine (what I have myself earlier labelled 'property-particulars' when I have dealt with the Phenomenalist interpretation), but also 'extended particulars'. The latter are, once again, the slow motions generating swifter ones. In light of this new terminology, a slow motion can be said to be an extended particular, which 'is a subjective bundling of certain sensibles along with the powers that generate those sensibles'.[11]

Despite providing such an ingenious interpretation of the ontology of the Secret Doctrine by relying on a modified version of the Causal Theory interpretation, Buckles claims that this interpretation is more of a problem than a solution for Protagoras' Secret Doctrine. In fact, Buckels argues that this metaphysics of particulars, both sensible and extended, cannot account for a central feature of the Secret Doctrine, that is, the symmetrical nature of the encounters of motions, both slow and swift. Buckles concludes that on his reading Plato was well aware of the problem and that he wanted to show that 'SD's (i.e. the Secret Doctrine) relational, subjective ontology requires a non-relational, objective underpinning, one which, furthermore, is relatively stable rather than an ever-changing process'.[12] I take Buckels' final point as evidence of a wider ontological problem, that is, the one that needs to explain property-particulars as ontologically dependent on extended particulars, or, said otherwise, how it is possible to develop a two-tier metaphysics of tropes where some are taken to be more ontologically fundamental than others. What I am to do in the next sections is to offer a less problematic outcome for the ontology of Protagoras' Secret Doctrine, thus arguing for an interpretation where a two-tier ontology of tropes is indeed theoretically possible. I will do so by looking at Vasubandhu's *Treasury of Metaphysics*, where the great Buddhist philosopher sketches an ontology of temporary dharmas that has remarkably close resemblances with the ontology of Protagoras' Secret Doctrine.

Vasubandhu's dharmas

For our own purposes here, we shall focus on the theory of dharmas as this is reconstructed in one of the most famous texts of Buddhist philosophy, Vasubandhu's *Abhidharmakośa*.[13] Vasubandhu's *Treasury of Metaphysics* (one of the possible translations of the original title) is a central text in the Buddhist tradition of the Abhidharma.[14] It develops a full ontology of dharmas, which are to be understood as the fundamental constituents of reality. But what is a dharma or what are the possible equivalents of the concept into a Western philosophical terminology is hard to say with precision. Let us get some hints by Vasubandhu himself.

First, dharmas are what we are left with after mereological decomposition and conceptual analysis. Vasubandhu makes the examples of the jug and the water:

(D) The idea of a jug ends when the jug is broken; the idea of water ends when, in the mind, one analyzes the water. The jug and the water, and all that resembles them, exist relatively. The rest exist absolutely (4.4).

He further comments:

(E) If the idea of a thing disappears when this thing is broken into pieces, then this thing has relative existence (*samvrtisat*); for example, a jug: the idea of a jug disappears when it is reduced to pieces. If the idea of a thing disappears when this thing is dissipated, or broken to pieces, by the mind, then this thing should be regarded as having relative existence; for example, water (4.4).

Something, like the jug or the chariot, which borrows its nature and existence from its parts is not a dharma – composite objects cannot be dharmas. Their existence is only relative. At the same time, the very idea of water disappears after conceptual analysis, so water cannot be a dharma. What we normally understand as composite objects such as jugs, chariots, tables and chairs have not only relative existence but are best seen as aggregates of more fundamental elements, such as dharmas, which on the contrary have ultimate existence and are atomic, that is, with no parts.[15]

Dharmas then must be not composite and are what is to be found as remaining after conceptual analysis. One is here tempted to take dharmas as a sort of Democritean atoms, that is, the ultimate physical elements of which reality is composed. But this would be misleading, because Vasubandhu does offer a compelling argument against physical atomism; dharmas in fact are said to exist in space but are not extended spatially. I may condense his argument along these lines. Atomic unities must aggregate to form bigger, macroscopic objects. If this is the case, individual atoms must touch one another in two ways: if they touch on their respective side, this will mean that all the aggregate of atoms purported to form a new, macroscopic object will collapse into a single spatial point, which will not be an atom anymore. Alternatively, when they touch to form a new object, if they do not share a side, they should – by necessity – be spatially distinct, hence spatially extended, so that they cannot be seen as being atoms anymore. In both cases, we are shown that the notion of atomic unity is problematic; a dharma cannot be a physical atom.[16]

Despite being what is left at a fundamental level after conceptual analysis and mereological decomposition, dharmas cannot after all be understood as the physical atoms of Democritean atomism. This does not mean that dharmas cannot be understood as sui-generis atoms. As Carpenter puts it: 'Vasubandhu's physical dharmas – the *paramānus* (that is, what we may call "atom") – must be dimensionless point-particle property-events'.[17] We shall come back to this point later in the chapter.

In addition to these characteristics, dharmas are wholly inserted in the causal order of the phenomenal world. As Vasubandhu puts it:

(F) All *dharmas* are *kdranahetu* (i.e. *reason of existence*) with regard to all, with the
exception of themselves.
A *dharma* is not a *kdranahetu* of itself.

With this exception, all *dharmas* are *kdranahetu* with regard to all other conditioned *dharmas*, because no *dharma* constitutes an obstacle to the arising of the *dharmas* susceptible of arising (2.50a).

Dharmas are causes of other subsequent dharmas (yet, not of themselves), which in turn arise as conditioned items. The world of phenomenal existence as we see it is simply a concatenation of caused dharmas. Not only are dharmas wholly internal to the causal process that constitutes the world out there, but they have also a temporary limited life, since each dharma lasts only for a moment. As Vasubandhu writes:

> (G) All conditioned things are momentary.
> What is understood by 'momentary' *(ksanika)*?
> *Ksana* means to perish immediately after having acquired its being (…).
> A conditioned thing does not exist beyond the acquisition of its being: it perishes on the spot where it arises; it cannot go from this spot to another (…).
> A conditioned thing perishes as soon as it arises; if it did not perish immediately, it would not perish later, since it would then remain the same. Since you admit that it perishes, you must admit that it immediately perishes. (4.2b–3b)

We have now some relevant information on dharmas: (1) they are momentary; (2) they are the product of causes and themselves causing other dharmas; (3) they are what is left after conceptual analysis and mereological decomposition; (4) they are atomic in space and time but they are not physical atoms as traditionally conceived of in ancient Greek philosophy. In canonical Abhidharma ontology, dharmas are thus characterized by all the four features listed above and are taken to be the primary elements of existence.[18] But how can we conceive of them in more straightforward philosophical terms?

Dharmas as tropes

In what remains the most perceptive analysis of the meaning and role of dharmas in the philosophy of Vasubandhu and, by extension, in Buddhist philosophy, Theodor Stcherbatsky remarks (echoing Vasubandhu) that 'its (i.e., a dharma's) inmost nature remains a riddle'.[19] Yet, Stcherbatsky provides us with a very illuminating philosophical account of the nature of dharmas by highlighting how dharmas strictly adhere to the three main marks of existence for Buddhists, that is, impermanence, instability, lack of stable ontological determination (*anitya, duhkha, anātman*).[20] We are going to meet again these three hallmarks of existence when we deal with the thought of Pyrrho in Chapter 4. Stcherbatsky explains the lack of stable ontological determination of dharmas by claiming that the Abhidharma schools denied any difference between the idea of a substance and that of a quality. He writes: '[for the Buddhists], there is no inherence of qualities in substance, in this respect all real elements are equally independent (…). All sense-data (*rūpa*) are substances in the sense that there is no stuff they belong to (…). Beside these sense-data there is absolutely nothing the name could be applied to'.[21] The main point here is that dharmas do not inhere in anything more fundamental than themselves, because there is no real ontological substratum to inhere to. For this reason, dharmas are what is left after conceptual analysis and mereological decomposition: they are the fundamental elements of reality.

Stcherbatsky notes that to make full sense of the Buddhist ontology of dharmas, we should link their lack of determination to their being unstable and impermanent. On dharmas as being unstable, he notes that the underlying idea is that dharmas are in a perpetual state of motion whose final aim is their extinction and dying away. This instability is closely related to impermanence, since an unstable item is doomed to be impermanent.[22] I now quote a famous passage by Stcherbatsky about the cinematographic conception of reality that somehow sums up the kernel of the Buddhist ontology of dharmas:

> The elements of existence are momentary appearances, momentary flashings into the phenomenal world out of an unknown source. Just as they are disconnected, so to say, in breadth, not being linked together by any pervading substance, just so are they disconnected in depth or in duration, since they last only one single moment (ksana). They disappear as soon as they appear, in order to be followed the next moment by another momentary existence. Thus a moment becomes a synonym of an element (dharma), two moments are two different elements. An element becomes something like a point in time-space (…). The elements do not change, but disappear, the world becomes a cinema. Disappearance is the very essence of existence; what does not disappear does not exist. A cause for the Buddhists was not a real cause but a preceding moment, which likewise arouse out of nothing in order to disappear into nothing.[23]

As has been more recently highlighted by Jan Westerhoff, in this conception of reality the world is best understood as a three-dimensional film projection, in which each dharma follows another one, like frames in a movie. It is our perception, which lacks the capacity to see deeper into the structure of reality, which sees objects where there is, in fact, none.[24] The cinematographic conception of reality that is implicit in the Buddhist ontology of dharmas does take into account all their features as we have reconstructed them briefly in this chapter. Dharmas are ontologically fundamental, momentary, atomic, impermanent, unstable, lacking any stable ontological determination (we shall come back to causation later). While he provides such a careful analysis of the role and meaning of dharmas in Vasubandhu's *Treasury*, Stcherbatsky ultimately interprets them in terms of Russellian sense-data.[25] In light of the kind of understanding of dharmas as the one provided here, recent interpreters have – and rightly so – taken them to be something very close to the tropes of contemporary metaphysics. After all, a dharma can be indeed taken to identify *this* red colour here, which is something different from *that* read colour there. Dharmas cannot be bearers of properties since they *are* properties. In short, they are property-particulars, that is, tropes, with the idea that every particular is different (again, *this* red colour is different from *that* red colour). Because dharmas are immersed into a chain of processes, they can also be conceived as property-particular *events*. Each dharma is an atomic, time-limited episode of existence.[26]

Dharmas, causation and Protagoras' Secret Doctrine

We are now ready to get back to Protagoras' Secret Doctrine. The ontology of dharmas as this is shown to operate in Vasubandhu's *Treasury* is astonishingly similar to the one depicted in Protagoras' Secret Doctrine. In both, there is a metaphysics of processes at work, which shows that everything is in motion, with nothing to endure beyond the very limits of its momentary existence. Nothing exists beyond these episodes of momentary existence, which again in both cases can be interpreted as property-particulars moments, or indeed property-particular events. In both Protagoras' Secret Doctrine and Vasubandhu's *Treasury*, material objects as we usually conceive of them are totally eliminated and replaced by these property-particular events: *dharmas* in Vasubandhu's Treasury, *twin-events* in Protagoras' Secret Doctrine.

If we now look at the role of causation in Vasubandhu's theory of dharmas, we shall find a replication of the hermeneutical scheme that we have seen at work when we have tried to understand Protagoras' Secret Doctrine, that is, the one centred on the Causal Theory and the Phenomenalist interpretations. Again, this shows how extraordinarily similar the two ontologies of dharmas and twins are. As briefly illustrated, dharmas are immersed in a world of processes where causation plays a key-role. Individual dharmas are autonomous space-time points, which are connected by the law of causation, so that one dharma actually causes the existence of another. In terms of momentariness, each moment is caused by – and follows – the preceding one. The inescapability of causation in Vasubandhu's ontology of dharmas means that, in comparison with Protagoras' Secret Doctrine, it would favour the Casual Theory interpretation. In its revised version, the Causal Theory interpretation in fact highlights that slow motions cause swift motions and, hence, the twins of perceptions and perceived properties (that is, property-particulars or tropes). In both Vasubandhu's theory of dharmas and in Protagoras' Secret Doctrine as this is understood in the Causal Theory reading, causation is central and responsible for the creation and birth of new property-particulars.

Not all interpreters of Vasubandhu's theory of dharmas, however, are happy to recognize an absolute centrality to the laws of causation in the world-processes. In fact, while surely not rejecting the importance of causation all together in the ontology of dharmas, some interpreters highlight that each dharma may perish on its own, that is, it may die out for internal reasons once its existential power is exhausted. More than causation, it is this internal exhaustion of each dharma that explains the actual birth of new dharmas, somehow generated out of their fresher and momentary existential powers, in the chain of processes that is the world out there.[27] If read in light of Protagoras' Secret Doctrine, this understanding of Vasuandhu's ontology of dharmas does seem to have strong analogies with the Phenomenalist Interpretation of the former. The Phenomenalist interpretation rejects the role of causation in the ontology of the Secret Doctrine, while highlighting at the same time the fact that each twin, each property-particular somehow follows the preceding one, in an uninterrupted process of tropes.[28]

The double reading of Vasubandhu's theory of dharmas (causation versus internal exhaustion) corresponds to the two readings of Protagoras' Secret Doctrine, that is, the Casual Theory and the Phenomenalist interpretations. This confirms not only the close analogy between the two ontological theories, but it also shows that both theories may oscillate between the two alternative readings because of an internal tension. Both readings are philosophically legitimate, in so far as they both offer a coherent ontology of processes. The philosopher may be happy to take both readings on board and then decide which is best from a theoretical point of view. The historical exegete may want to press further the question and see which one best suits the text, either Plato's *Theaetetus* or Vasubandhu's *Treasury*. My next and final move is a middle way between the philosopher and the historian since I aim to show that the problem Buckles sees as arising for Protagoras even on the ground of a revised Causal Theory interpretation does not arise for Vasubandhu. This shows that Buckels' problem is not a conceptual one that any ontology of tropes, such as Protagoras' Secret Doctrine and/or Vasubandhu's theory of dharmas, must be faced with.

A two-tier ontology of tropes

As seen above, Buckels argues that Protagoras' ontology of property-particulars, both sensible and extended, cannot account for a central feature of the Secret Doctrine, that is, the symmetrical nature of the encounters of motions, both slow and swift. He adds that according to him Plato aimed to show that 'SD's relational, subjective ontology requires a non-relational, objective underpinning, one which, furthermore, is relatively stable rather than an everchanging process'.[29] As I noted above, I read Buckels' worry about symmetrical encounters as an example of a wider ontological problem, that is, the one that explains how property-particulars can be ontologically dependent upon extended particulars, or, said otherwise, how it possible to develop a two-tier metaphysics of tropes, where some are taken to be more ontologically fundamental than others.

On some interpretations, in his theory of dharmas Vasubandhu seems to offer a plausible way to explain how in an ontology of tropes, some are taken to be more fundamental than others; that is, Vasubandhu offers some argument to show how some less fundamental tropes can supervene on more fundamental ones.[30] Vasubandhu divides matter (or physical form, *rūpa*) into two sub-groups: the four great elements (air, earth, fire and water) and the derived form, which includes all physical entities such as colours, perceptions (that is, all the property-particulars we mentioned earlier).[31] There are two ways to understand the nature of the four great elements: either they are tiny, fundamental particles (atoms) of air, earth, fire and water (and something else);[32] or these four elements are best understood as basic tropes.[33] This dispute does not need to concern us here, because in both interpretations, what is at issue is that the basic elements (atomic items or fundamental tropes) are responsible for the existence of less fundamental tropes, the property-particulars of our perpetual experience. This point is clearly stated by Vasubandhu:

> (H) The four primary elements are causes of the derived elements – colour, taste, etc. – in five ways, in the quality of *janana, nisraya, pratisthd, upastambha,* and *upabrmhanahe*
>
> *Jananahetu* or generating cause, because the derived elements arise from them, like a child from his parents.
>
> *Nisrayahetu* or tutelage cause, because the *bhautikas,* once arisen, submerge their influence, as a monk is under the tutelage of his Acarya and his Upadhyaya.
>
> *Pratisthdhetu* or supporting cause, because the derived elements are supported by them, as a picture is supported by a wall. *Upastambhahetu* or maintaining cause, because the primary elements are the cause of the non-interruption of the derived elements. *Upabrmhanahetu* or growth cause, because the primary elements are the cause of the development of the derived elements.
>
> This means that the primary elements (*bhutas*) are, with regard to the derived elements (*bhautikas*), the cause of arising (*janmahetu*), the cause of transformation (*vikarahetu*), the supporting cause (*ddhara – hetu*),the cause of duration (*sthitihetu*), and the cause of development.[34]

Vasubandhu's view closely mirrors the explanation of causation that does the work in Buckels' revised version of the Causal Theory interpretation. In Vasubandhu's theory of dharmas/tropes, we have the great elements doing the work that Buckles' 'extended particulars' (or slow motions with powers) do in Protagoras' Secret Doctrine. Vasubandhu's primary/great elements and Protagoras' slow motions are the more fundamental tropes that cause the existence of less fundamental tropes, that is, property-particulars such as

Vasubandhu's dharmas and Protagoras' twins (or swift motions). Vasubandhu's reference in the passage above to the generating cause (parents generating offspring as a metaphor for derived form) is also literally very close to the image that is at the heart of the Stage Two development in Protagoras' Secret Doctrine: parents (that is, slow motions) generate their offspring (that is, swift motions) that, in the Theaetetus' case, are always twins.

Vasubandhu's theory of dharmas therefore has very close analogies with Protagoras' Secret Doctrine. Both theories, at least on some plausible interpretations, offer an ontology of tropes that is original and unprecedented in both Greek and Buddhist thought. At the same time, Vasubandhu's theory of dharmas provides a two-tier ontology of tropes that can explain how less fundamental tropes are generated by more fundamental ones. This two-tier ontology gives us a solution to the problem that Buckles takes to vitiate Protagoras' Secret Doctrine even when interpreted under the benevolent light of the revised Causal Theory interpretation. There is a plausible philosophical way to explain why slow motions need to be more fundamental items than swift ones and how the former can be understood as generating the latter. It is not thus the case that in an ontology of tropes such as the one sketched in Protagoras' Secret Doctrine and in Vasubandhu's *Treasury* a two-tier ontology of tropes is conceptually unworkable. Given the strict philosophical analogies between Vasubandhu's theory of dharmas and the doctrine of perceptual twins in Protagoras' Secret Doctrine, it may well be claimed that a two tier-ontology for slow and swift motions (with the latter being supervenient on the former) is indeed possible for the latter too, with Buckels' problem of symmetrical encounter being put aside.

3

Gorgias and Nāgārjuna on nihilism

After having dealt with Protagoras' Secret Doctrine and Vasubandhu's theory of dharmas in Chapters 1 and 2, in this chapter we are going to deal with an important strand of nihilistic arguments to be found in the works of two philosophers who have so far never been studied comparatively: the other great sophist of Ancient Greece, Gorgias, and the Buddhist monk Nāgārjuna.[1] The aim of the chapter is mainly exegetical. First, the arguments Gorgias sets forth in the first section of his treatise *On What Is Not* are carefully examined. In this way the reader is offered some help in untangling the intricacies of the first serious defence of metaphysical nihilism in the history of Greek thought, no matter what Gorgias' original intents were. After having reconstructed Gorgias' moves in the first section of *On What Is Not*, the chapter shows how the nihilist arguments Gorgias uses mostly feature, under a new light, in the philosophy of emptiness developed by Nāgārjuna. The chapter ends with a hermeneutical suggestion: that is, to replace traditional 'sceptical' interpretations of Gorgias and Nāgārjuna with an alternative one that takes them as possibly committed to nihilism.

Both Gorgias (475–380BC) and Nāgārjuna (most probably first/second century AD) are philosophers whose views are differently interpreted in the scholarship. Gorgias is often seen as the father of rhetoric who was mainly interested in showing, in the sophistication of his works, the power of persuasion while overall lacking a serious philosophical scope. When one is attributed to him, it has more to do with epistemology, not with metaphysics or metaphysical nihilism.[2] On the other hand, Nāgārjuna, the second Buddha, is indeed a central figure in Buddhist metaphysical debates and, more generally, in Buddhist philosophy *tout court*. Nāgārjuna insists that his philosophy of emptiness is to be read as a Middle Way between nihilism and eternalism.[3]

Overall, then, metaphysical nihilism (understood as the view that *nihil est*, i.e., that nothing is)[4] is not a view that can be easily attributed to either Gorgias or Nāgārjuna. Yet, if we take the first section of Gorgias' treatise on *What Is Not* at face value, without speculating on the possible reasons for which Gorgias wrote it, we find compelling arguments that can easily be read as arguing for nihilism. At the same time, Gorgias' (nihilist) arguments have remarkably close analogies with other arguments set forth by Nāgārjuna in some of his main works, arguments that, again, can well be read along nihilist lines. This makes neither Gorgias nor Nāgārjuna as philosophers *per se* immediately professing nihilist views; yet there seems to be an analogy of arguments in the main works of these two philosophers that is best understood as pointing towards nihilism. We now turn to the philosophical reconstruction and analysis of these arguments.

Gorgias' On What Is Not: *Structure and argument*

Gorgias' *On What Is Not or On Nature* (*Peri Tou Mē Ontos ē Peri Phuseōs*: henceforth, *PTMO*) has not been preserved in its original form. We are, however, lucky enough to have two detailed accounts of Gorgias' work, one provided by the sceptical philosopher Sextus Empiricus and another preserved in a treatise entitled *On Melissus, Xenophanes and Gorgias* (henceforth, *MXG*). The author of the treatise is unknown (hence we use the general label 'Anonymous'), but he is likely to be someone belonging to Aristotle's school.[5] Despite having two detailed accounts of Gorgias' *PTMO*, we are further saddened by the bad state in which some part of *MXG* is preserved. Yet, thanks to Roberta Ioli, we now have a reliable critical edition of Gorgias' work.[6]

Gorgias' *PTMO* argues for three main theses: (1) nothing is; (2) even if it were, it could not be known; (3) if it were and could be known, it could not be communicated to anyone. Both Anonymous and Sextus begin their accounts by reporting these three theses.[7] They both move on to deal with Gorgias' first claim that nothing is. Yet, they do so in diverse ways. Anonymous splits his dealing with Gorgias' view that nothing is into two separate demonstrations, labelled respectively as Gorgias' proper logos (*idios apodeixis* or *prōton logos*) and dialectical logos (*sunthetikē apodeixis* or *deuteros logos*). On the other hand, Sextus presents Gorgias' claims by following the tripartite scheme (e.g., the trilemma, an argument with three different options on the table), which is typical of his (Sextus') sceptical argumentations.[8]

To compare and deal with these two accounts of Gorgias' *PTMO* is difficult enough even when one has both written down, but it becomes exhaustingly impossible when, as it often happens in scholarly articles, only short passages are given, with the bulk of the text summarized in different footnotes. For the sake of clarity, I shall provide the Anonymous' and Sextus' accounts in full, dividing them into a list of numbered Testimonies (**T**). For this chapter's purposes, we shall focus on the dialectical logos of the *PTMO*.

Gorgias' Argument against Generation and Eternity

Gorgias' dialectical logos puts forward four arguments that have played ever since a crucial role in the philosophical defence of nihilism. Both Anonymous and Sextus centre Gorgias' dialectical argument around two main antinomies: Generated/Ungenerated (or Eternal); One/Many. Anonymous provides two further arguments about movement that are not to be found explicitly in Sextus.

As for the antinomy Generated/Ungenerated (*Argument against Generation and Eternity*), Anonymous and Sextus reconstruct Gorgias' argument respectively as follows:

Anonymous:

> **T1** After this argument he says: if [scil. something] is, it is either ungenerated or generated. And if it is ungenerated, he accepts by Melissus' axioms that it is unlimited. But the unlimited could not be anywhere.[9] For it is neither in itself nor in something else: for in this way they would be two or more [scil. unlimiteds], the one within and the one within which. But nothing is that would be nowhere, according to Zeno's argument about place. For this reason, it is not ungenerated, and yet it is not generated either. (*MXG* 979b20–25)

T2 For nothing could come to be either out of what is or out of what is not. For if what is changed, it would no longer be what is, just as, if what is not came to be, it would no longer be something that is not. Nor certainly could it come to be from what is not.[10] For if what is not is not, nothing would come to be from nothing. And if what is not is, it could not come to be from what is not, for precisely the same reason that it does not come to be from what is. If then it is necessary, if something is, that it be either ungenerated or generated, and these are both <impossible>, then it is impossible too that anything be. (*MXG* 979b26–34)

Sextus:

T3: And again: the existent is not either. For if what is is, it is either eternal, or generated, or at the same time eternal and generated. But it is neither eternal, nor generated, nor both, as we shall show. So what is is not. (*M.* 7.68)

T4 For if what is is eternal (for this is where one must start from), it has no beginning. For everything that comes to be has some beginning, while what is eternal, being ungenerated, has not had a beginning. Not having a beginning, it is unlimited. And if it is unlimited, it is nowhere. For if it is somewhere, then what it is in is different from it, and in this way what is, being enclosed within something, will no longer be unlimited. For what encloses is larger than what is enclosed, while nothing is larger than the unlimited, so that the unlimited is not somewhere. And again: it is not enclosed within itself either. For the 'in which' and the 'in it' will be identical, and what is will become two, place and body (for the 'in which' is a place, and the 'in it' is a body). But this is quite absurd. Therefore what is is not in itself either. So that if what is is eternal, it is unlimited; if it is unlimited, it is nowhere; and if it is nowhere, it is not. Therefore if what is is eternal, it is absolutely not something that is. (*M.* 7.68–70)

T5 And again: what is cannot come to be either. For if it has come to be, it has come to be generated either out of what is or out of what is not. But it has not come to be out of what is (for if it is something that is, it has not come to be but already is) nor out of what is not (for what is not is not able to generate anything because what is generative of something must necessarily have a share in existence). So what is is not generated either. (*M.* 7.71)

T6 In the same way, it is not both, eternal and generated, at the same time. For these abolish each other, and if what is is eternal, it has not come to be, and if it has come to be, it is not eternal. Therefore, if what is is neither eternal nor generated nor both, what is could not be. (*M.* 7.72)

If what is is ungenerated, it must be unlimited – on the ground of Melissus' argument, who claimed that what is ungenerated is eternal, that is, it has no (temporal) beginning or end.[11] Since the ungenerated is eternal, it is also infinite, that is, it has no boundaries (in space).[12] If what is is thus unlimited (both in time and space), it must be one, since if there were two unlimited items, it would mean that one limits the other, which is not possible.[13] So, the ungenerated is unlimited as well as infinite. But we cannot locate infinity anywhere around us; infinity is nowhere to be found. But, as Zeno seems to have claimed, what is not to be found anywhere is not.[14] So, nothing is.

By relying on a battery of arguments about generation, eternity, unlimitedness and infinity that Melissus set out to argue for the unity and existence of being, with the support of Zeno's paradox on places Gorgias reverses Melissus' arguments to show that after all nothing is. In his version of the same argument, without mentioning Melissus or Zeno, Sextus uses similar arguments to show that for Gorgias what is unlimited is not (compare **T1** with **T4**). The same similarity of arguments between Anonymous and Sextus is to be found when they deal with the second horn of the dilemma, that is, generation (compare **T2** and **T5**). What comes into existence can be generated either from what is or from what is not. In the former case, it would mean that to generate something different, what is should be by necessity modified and transformed into what is not – something that is not possible. On the other hand, generation from what is not is impossible, because nothing would originate from nothing. So again, nothing is.

Gorgias' Argument against Monism and Plurality

As for the antinomy One/Many (*Argument against Monism and Plurality*), both Anonymous and Sextus provide the same logical pattern in tackling the issue of monism and plurality. Here are the two versions of Gorgias' argument:

Anonymous:

T7 Again, if [*scil.* something] is, he says, it is one or more. But if it is neither one nor many, then it would be nothing. And it [could not be] one because it would be incorporeal, and [what is incorporeal, not] possessing magnitude, [is nothing], as by Zeno's argument. But if it is [not] one, it must [definitely] be nothing; for, if [there is no one], neither [can] many [be]. But if, [as Gorgias says], it is neither [one] nor many, then nothing is. (*MXG* 979b35–980a1)

Sextus:

T8 And in a different way: if it is, it is either one or multiple. But it is neither one nor many, as will be proven; so what is is not. For if it is one, it is either a [scil. discrete] quantity, or continuous, or a magnitude, or a body. But whichever of these it is, it is not one: if it is constituted as a quantity, it will be divided; if it is continuous, it will be cut; in the same way, if it is thought as a magnitude, it will not be indivisible; and if it turns out to be a body, it will be triple, for it will have length, breadth, and depth. But it is absurd to say that what is is not any of these: so what is is not one. And again: it is not multiple either. For if it is not one, it is not multiple either: for a plurality is a composition of unities, and that is why, if the one is destroyed, the plurality is destroyed together with it. That neither what is is, nor what is not, is evident from these arguments. (*M.* 7.73–4)

If something is, it must be incorporeal, since Gorgias seems here to follow Melissus in taking being as having no body.[15] But, following Zeno,[16] if what is is incorporeal and has no magnitude (because it is not a body), it is nothing. Sextus adds spatial and temporal continuity as well as quantity to the list of the properties of the One being discussed, with the same outcome to be reached: nothing is. At the same time, both Anonymous and Sextus argue, if the one is not, many cannot be either. A plurality is the sum of unities; when the latter are not, the former is not either.

Gorgias' Argument against Motion: Against Change and Division

While the arguments about generation, eternity, monism and plurality feature in both *MXG* and Sextus as the bulk of Gorgias' dialectical argument, there is another argument that Gorgias put forward in his defence of nihilism that is to be found in the *MXG* only. This is the *Argument against Motion*, which can be further divided into the *Argument against Change* and the *Argument against Division*.[17] As for the former, Anonymous writes:

> **T9** He says that it could not move either. For if it [*scil.* the thing in question] moved, it would no longer be in the same way, but on the one hand it would not be, and on the other what is not would have come to be. (*MXG* 980a1–4)

Gorgias' argument starts off with an argument against motion understood as ontological 'change'. For, as Gorgias says, if something moves from its condition of ontological stability to undergo a modification, that thing would no longer be the same thing as before: on the one hand, it would not be anymore, and on the other what is not would have come to be. So, motion, when it is understood as ontological change, is impossible.[18]

As for the *Argument against Division*, Anonymous writes:

> **T10** Moreover, if it moves and is transported, not being continuous, it is divided, and <where> what is <is divided,> it is not: so that if it moves everywhere, it is divided everywhere. But if this is so, then it is not in any place [or: nor at all]. For where there is division, there is lack of what is – he says 'to be divided' instead of 'void,' as is written in what are called the arguments of Leucippus. (*MXG* 980a5–8)

Gorgias seems once again to rely on the Eleatic assumption that being cannot move because otherwise this would imply divisibility.[19] Gorgias' argument is hard to reconstruct in detail. It could run along these lines: if something moves, it is no longer continuous and is thus divided, which means it is not anymore – because what is cannot be divided. At the same time, what is divided is equivalent to void, which is equivalent to not being. If it moves everywhere, it will mean that it is divided, and so it is nowhere to be found. These last two arguments against motion give us a glimpse into an elaborate debate about motion, monism, plurality, being and nothingness that involved the Atomists, the Eleatics (especially Zeno) and Gorgias. For the purposes of the present chapter, we shall not delve into that debate.[20] It is enough for us to highlight that the battery of argument in defence of nihilism that Gorgias puts forward in his dialectical logos are to be found, revised and redeveloped, in Nāgārjuna's philosophy of emptiness.

Nāgārjuna and nihilism

Let us now turn to Nāgārjuna, the founder and main figure of the Madhyamaka school.[21] Nāgārjuna is the philosopher whose name has often been strongly associated with nihilism. Yet, there is no scholarly consensus on Nāgārjuna's endorsement of nihilism. First, Nāgārjuna is taken to say that he has no view to offer, his philosophy mainly consisting in a sort of refutation of all views.[22] He also claims that his philosophy of emptiness is a Middle Way between the two extremes of annihilation and eternalism.[23] For Nāgārjuna, all things are empty (śūnya), that is, they are devoid of intrinsic essence (svabhāva). Some, indeed many interpreters have taken emptiness, although not equivalent to it, to lead naturally to nihilism. Since all (dependently arising) entities are devoid of intrinsic essence, nothing seems to exist.[24] Nāgārjuna retorts that it is emptiness itself that explains the actual existence of all entities. Entities exist as dependently arising items (pratītyasamutpanna) and as such they are empty of independent existence. Yet, they exist as arising upon causes and conditions. If you deny emptiness, that is, the fact that entities arise upon causes and conditions, Nāgārjuna claims, you deny that dependent entities exist.[25] Yet, the list of philosophers who both in antiquity and in more recent times take Nāgārjuna' theory of emptiness as invariably leading to nihilism is long.[26] As Burton has claimed, 'Nāgārjuna might think that he treads the Middle Way, but perhaps in fact he has taken a wrong turning', that is, Nāgārjuna is, consciously or not, a nihilist.[27]

Of course, the millennial dispute about the real nature of Nāgārjuna's Middle Way cannot be settled in the context of this chapter. Yet for our own purposes here, it is enough to highlight that, despite Nāgārjuna's own protests, some nihilistic understandings of his philosophy seem possible and that such understanding has been popular both in ancient and more recent times. We now turn to some specific arguments in Nāgārjuna's main works that can be read along nihilistic lines and that also show a great degree of analogy with Gorgias' 'nihilistic' arguments (as these are illustrated in the dialectical section of the *PTMO*). I am not claiming that the nihilist interpretation of Nāgārjuna's arguments that I am going to offer in the next sections is the only way to read his arguments. My claim is that a nihilist reading is, however, indeed possible, and this is even more the case when the close analogy between Gorgias' 'nihilist' arguments and Nāgārjuna's own ones is taken in due account.

Let me give some brief details on those works by Nāgārjuna that are to be dealt with in the following sections. Much is taken from Nāgārjuna's main work, *Mūlamadhyamakakārikā* (*The Treatise on the Middle Way=MMK*), the fundamental text of the Madyhamaka school. It consists of twenty-seven chapters in verses in Sanskrit. Given its importance, *MMK* has been widely commentated in both Indian and Tibetan traditions.[28] I shall also rely on *Śūnyatāsaptakārikā* (*The Seventy Stanzas on Emptiness=ŚS*), which is extant only in its Tibetan text, the Sanskrit version being lost and with no available Chinese translation of it. *The Seventy Stanzas* consists of seventy-three stanzas (in verses).[29] I also quote a passage from the first part of Nāgārjuna's *Ratnāvalī* (*The Precious Garland=RA*), an important work where Nāgārjuna places the main tenets of his philosophy into a broader, also practical context.[30]

Nāgārjuna's Arguments against Causation and Eternalism

In close dialogue and contrast with rival Abhidharma schools, Nāgārjuna aims at showing that all things are empty (*śūnya*) or devoid of intrinsic nature (*svabhāva*).[31] Since Nāgārjuna aims for comprehensiveness in his attempt to demonstrate that all is devoid of *svabhāva*, he produces a substantial number of arguments in support of his claim, some of them mirroring closely the sort of arguments that Gorgias employs in the dialectical logos of the *PTMO*.

Let us start with the *Argument against Generation and Eternity*. While Gorgias spoke of generation, Nāgārjuna refers to causation, a central concept of his philosophy.[32] Nāgārjuna sees causation and existence by *svabhāva* as truly incompatible.[33] What is understood as being caused by something else has no intrinsic existence on its own – Nāgārjuna claims. As he puts it:

> **T11** It is not correct to say that intrinsic nature is produced
> by means of causes and conditions.
> An intrinsic nature that was produced by causes and conditions would be a product.

> But how could there ever be an intrinsic nature that is a product?
> For intrinsic nature is not adventitious, not is it dependent
> on something else. (*MMK* 15:1–2)

The *svabhāva* of something that has been newly caused cannot already be present in the causes and conditions that produced the new thing. If this were the case, causation would be pointless: why start a fire to obtain heat if there were already heat in the fuel? It does seem that when we have *svabhāva*, there can be no causation whatsoever. Causation and intrinsic nature are mutually exclusive. Because causation cannot bring about true existence and since causation is everywhere to be found around us, nothing with intrinsic nature seems to exist for Nāgārjuna. He begins *MMK* by declaring:

> **T12** Not from itself, not from another, not from both, nor
> without cause:
> Never in any way is there any existing thing that has arisen. (*MMK* 1:1)[34]

According to these celebrated verses, there are four possible logical ways in which existing things may be thought to be caused/arisen:[35] (1) by itself; (2) by something else; (3) by both itself and something else; (4) by nothing at all. Nāgārjuna rejects all these four possibilities, arguing that anything that exists by *svabhāva* cannot originate from anything.[36] While Nāgārjuna's *Argument against Causation* can be read as reshaping Gorgias' *Argument against Generation* (see **TT 2&5**) by highlighting the close linkage between the fundamental category of intrinsic essence and (the lack of) causation, there are other arguments by Nāgārjuna that can be read in parallel with Gorgias' argument against eternity.

The *Argument against Eternity* that Gorgias advances in the dialectical logos rests on the idea that since we cannot locate the infinite (which is also ungenerated, unlimited and eternal) anywhere, nothing is (see **TT 1&4**). It is now to be shown that Gorgias' argument has close analogies with Nāgārjuna's *Argument against Eternalism*. More in particular, Nāgārjuna's Middle Way can be understood as a Middle Path between annihilationism and eternalism – indeed this is what he claims his philosophy to be.[37] While as seen it is widely disputed in the scholarship how we could take Nāgārjuna's philosophy of emptiness as a middle way between the two extremes of annihilationism and eternalism, one thing can be said with no danger to be refuted: Nāgārjuna does argue against eternalism.[38] There are plenty of places in the *MMK* in which he does that.³⁹ Let us focus briefly on the final section of *MMK* 15, the chapter where he deals most extensively with intrinsic essence. After having shown that both intrinsic nature and extrinsic (i.e., borrowed: *parabhāva*) nature are nowhere to be found, Nāgārjuna writes:

> **T13** If something existed by essential nature, then there
> would not be the nonexistence of such a thing.
> For it never holds that there is the alteration of essential nature. (*MMK* 15:8)

With the proviso to take 'essential nature' as equivalent to 'intrinsic nature', the argument here is something along the following lines: if there is something that exists (because of its *svabhāva*), this would mean that it could not stop existing under any circumstance. This, in turn, will mean that it is eternal. Considering the Buddha's teaching, we must however reject eternalism because it is not true of things. There is nothing in the world that does not undergo any change. Wherever we look at, we find things such as material objects and selves as permanently undergoing ontological changes.⁴⁰ This means that nothing is eternal. Given the strict linkage Nāgārjuna draws between eternalism and existence, if nothing is eternal, nothing with intrinsic essence seems to exist:

> **T14** If there were existence in itself of things, there would be eternalism; if
> there is non-being, there is necessarily annihilation.
> When there is being, these two [dogmas] occur. Therefore
> [one should] not accept being. (*ŚS* 21)

In both Nāgārjuna's *Argument against Eternalism* and in Gorgias' *Argument against Eternity*, intrinsic/true existence and eternity are linked, together with unchangeability. Since we cannot locate (the) infinity (of eternity) anywhere, Gorgias claimed that we should conclude that nothing is. As for Nāgārjuna, eternalism implies intrinsic essence. Eternalism is not true, as the Buddha taught. We can legitimately conclude that nothing exists by *svabhāva*.

Nāgārjuna's Arguments against Plurality and Atomism

While they diverge on the role of causation in the ontological process, both Abhidharma and Madhyamaka agree that composite material objects do not have intrinsic nature because they borrow their existence from that of the parts composing them. The traditional example is that of the chariot, whose existence is such that it is temporarily borrowed from the parts that compose it.[41] On the basis of this argument, then, composite objects do not have *svabhāva* – in short, they are conceptual fiction. This argument about composition seems to be implicit in Gorgias' *Arguments against Plurality and Monism* too: the existence of composite objects rests upon the real existence of the parts composing them. If the latter are not, Gorgias argues, also the former are not (see **TT 7&8**).

Gorgias draws this conclusion after having shown that nothing is one, that is, after having shown that also the atomic components of reality (when understood as partless unities) are not. How does Nāgārjuna conceive of partless entities? Nāgārjuna' strategy is to show that existing things are neither many nor one.[42] He writes:

> **T15** Composite and non-composite are not many, are not one, are not being, are not non-being [and] are not being-non-being. (*ŚS* 32)[43]

There is also a debated verse from the *Precious Garland*, which goes like this:

> **T16** No [atom] is simple, being many-sided; no atom is sideless (*nāpradeśaś*) [in so far as its connection with other atoms would, then, be impossible]; on the other hand, the idea of plurality is inconceivable without that of unity nor that of non-existence without that of existence. (*RA* 1:17; Tucci's translation)

Not only does Nāgārjuna here reiterate the point about plurality being pointless without unity – the same view that Gorgias highlights in his *Argument against Plurality*; Nāgārjuna also constructs an argument against partless entities aimed to show that unity is not either. The crucial term in **T16** is '*pradeśa*', which can mean 'part' – so that a most natural translation of *nāpradeśaś* (line 1 in T) is 'partless'. Tucci (Tucci 1934), however, translates is as 'sideless' because, quite correctly I think, he takes Nāgārjuna's argument in these verses as anticipating a well-known argument against atomism that Vasubandhu and the Yogācārins employed.[44] The argument goes along these lines: atomic unities must aggregate to form bigger, macroscopic objects. If this is the case, individual atoms must touch one another in two ways: if they touch on their respective side (*pradeśa*), this will mean that all the aggregate of atoms purported to form a new, macroscopic object will collapse into a single spatial point, which will not be an atom anymore. Alternatively, when they touch to form a new object, if they do not share a side, they should – by necessity – be spatially distinct, hence spatially extended, so that they cannot be seen as being atoms anymore. In both cases, we are shown that the notion of atomic unity is problematic and cannot account for how macroscopic objects arise from atomic entities. By relying on the notion of partless entities, we cannot show how plurality arises from unity. Both plurality and unity are best dispensed of.[45] If things are neither one nor many, well, they are empty of intrinsic essence:

> **T17** Since all things all together lack *svabhāva*, either in causes or conditions [or their] totality or separately, they are therefore empty (*śūnya*). (ŚS3)[46]

Again, one conceivable way to read the emptiness of things (when arising from totality or separation) is to think of them as non-existent: if things are neither one nor many (with the options of unicity and multiplicity to exhaust the logical space of all possibilities for one thing to be something under composition), well, we are left with one logical possibility: that arising things are nothing with intrinsic essence.

Nāgārjuna's Argument against Change

Remarkably close similarities, then, are to be found between Gorgias' and Nāgārjuna's *Arguments against Plurality, Monism and Atomism*. Let us move to the final argument of Gorgias' dialectical logos, that is, the *Argument against Motion*, which is further divided into the *Argument against Change* and the *Argument against Division*. Gorgias' *Argument against Change* was the following one (see **T9**): if something moves from its condition of ontological stability to undergo a modification, it would no longer be the same thing as before: on the one hand, it would not be anymore, and on the other what is not would have come to be, which is not possible. So, nothing really is.

As seen Gorgias' argument rests on an assumption that being is fully and completely homogeneous, that is, always identical to itself and undergoing no ontological change whatsoever. This view of being is shared by Nāgārjuna, who claims that what has *svabhāva* is ontologically unmodifiable. As he puts it:

> **T18** The world would be unproduced, unceased, and unchangeable,
> it would be devoid of its manifold appearances, if there were
> intrinsic nature. (*MMK* 24:38)⁴⁷

What exists by intrinsic essence – Nāgārjuna claims – cannot change in any respect and at any time; if age is something to be had by *svabhāva*, a young man could never become old:

> **T19** It is not correct to say that change pertains to the thing itself that is said to change or to what is distinct. For a youth does not age, nor does the aged one age. (*MMK* 13:5)

But we do grow old. So, one may well conclude, nothing exists by *svabhāva*, because everything keeps changing around us. The actual implication of nihilism about existing things seems to be explicit in the objection posed to Nāgārjuna by his opponent exactly in these verses of *MMK*:

> [Objection]: By the observation of change [it is to be inferred] the lack of intrinsic nature of things. There is no ultimately real existent that is without intrinsic nature, due to the emptiness of existents. (*MMK* 13:3a–4b)

It could not be true, the opponent argues, that all things are empty. If this were the case, there would be nothing to be empty, that is, nihilism would be true. To which objection Nāgārjuna replies that there could not be any change if there were things with intrinsic nature (*MMK* 13:4c–d). Again, the tension between a possibly nihilist reading of Nāgārjuna's arguments that seems natural for his opponents and his subsequent rebuttal of the charge of nihilism is present in these sections of the *MMK*. This shows, once again, that to take Nāgārjuna's arguments on change as ultimately leading to nihilism can be a plausible reading of what he seems to be saying here.

While there is a close parallelism between Gorgias' and Nāgārjuna's *Argument against Change*, much can also be said about the last argument Gorgias brings out in the dialectical logos, that is, the *Argument against Division*. While it can be claimed that this argument is a variation of the previous argument against monism and plurality, it is also true that Gorgias' arguments against divisibility and motion do refer to some arguments on space and time (most likely to be attributed to Zeno) that are still in need to be clarified. Most importantly, I think it could be shown how Zeno's arguments on motion, space and time played a significant role in the actual formulation of a nihilist trend in ancient philosophy – if indeed there was one, as this chapter claims. And once this is done, I suspect that close similarities will be found between those arguments and Nāgārjuna's *Argument against Motion* in *MMK* 2. This is the chapter of *Mūlamadhyamakakārikā* in which by showing that there is no going, no goer and no destination whatsoever, Nāgārjuna argues against the very possibility of motion.

There is no scholarly consensus on how to take the main arguments against motion Nāgārjuna develops in *MMK* 2: some commentators understand those arguments as Zenonian in style, content and inspiration, while others seem to provide an interpretation of them as arguments against ontological instantiation and change.[48] In both cases, there is scope for a closer look between Gorgias' *Argument against Motion* in the dialectical logos and Nāgārjuna's discussion of motion in *MMK* 2, to understand how they can be read as arguments that can have a nihilist interpretation.

Retrospect and conclusion

In the chapter it has been shown that in the dialectical logos of *PTMO* Gorgias develops four arguments that can be read as nihilist arguments: the *Arguments against Generation and Eternity, against Monism and Plurality, against Motion* (further divided in the *Argument against Change* and the *Argument against Division*). On his part, in his own works Nāgārjuna offers some other arguments that closely resemble Gorgias' four arguments. Nāgārjuna's arguments have been labelled, respectively, as *Arguments against Causation and Eternalism, against Plurality and Atomism, against Change*. All these arguments can be read along nihilist lines.

What does this analogy of arguments between Gorgias and Nāgārjuna show? First, it tells us that nihilist arguments were present in both ancient Greek and Buddhist philosophy, thus linking more closely the two philosophical traditions on a topic that has been often neglected in the history of ancient thought.[49] Secondly, and perhaps more importantly, it invites us to rethink the ways we can look at both Gorgias and Nāgārjuna. In this chapter, I have just stopped short of claiming that, although with different approaches, Gorgias and Nāgārjuna endorsed metaphysical nihilism. After all, the still dominant way to interpret Gorgias' works is to take them as skilful exhibitions of rhetorical display or as the crafted efforts of someone not primarily interested in philosophy, even less in metaphysics. But this approach is more prejudicial than one may think at first, because it makes us not fully appreciate, from a philosophical point of view, the sophisticated defence of nihilism that Gorgias does provide in the *PTMO*. It also makes us wrongly assume that metaphysical nihilism is somehow absent from the scene of ancient Greek philosophy. On the contrary, one of the aims of this book is to show some Greek thinkers such as Protagoras (as depicted in Plato's *Theaetetus*), the Cyrenaics and Pyrrho could be inscribed into a general tendency present in ancient philosophy that eliminated material objects (as we usually conceive of them) from the metaphysical apparatus of the world. In other words, what hermeneutical revision could we make to the history of Greek philosophy if we took Gorgias not only as a simple proposer of nihilist arguments for rhetorical or dialectical purposes but also as a *believer* in them too? In this way, Gorgias could profitably join a nihilist/eliminativist strand in ancient Greek metaphysics whose story is yet to be told.

The same refreshing perspective on Buddhist philosophy may be gained when we take a new 'nihilist' approach to Nāgārjuna. It is true, as we have briefly seen in the context of this chapter, that despite his own protests nihilist readings of Nāgārjuna are well present in the history of Buddhist philosophy, either ancient or contemporary. But it is also true that sceptical or dialectical interpretations of Nāgārjuna's thought remain popular: these interpretations take his arguments, including the 'nihilist' ones this chapter is concerned about, as a single part of wider two-part arguments aimed at showing that also the opposite position is to be rejected.[50] While the reading of Nāgārjuna as a thinker who directly or indirectly, consciously or less consciously, endorsed nihilism may have its own problems, the rival sceptical reading is still at odds at explaining how Nāgārjuna could have motivated his philosophy of emptiness in a coherent way. After all, Nāgārjuna says he has no views to defend. It is also true that, in a sort of (proto-)Wittgensteinian fashion, Nāgārjuna attempts to defend the special status of his statement about emptiness in a crucial section of the *Vigrahavyāvartanī*, hence throwing away the ladder after climbing on it. But I am not sure that his attempt is successful and cannot be charged with circularity.[51]

If we still want to take Nāgārjuna as a sceptic, why don't we look at Pyrrho, the founder of ancient scepticism? Like Nāgārjuna, Pyrrho refused to endorse any view, the tradition after him generating a full web of opposite arguments that were taken as invalidating each other. But as the next chapter will show, Pyrrho committed himself to at least one metaphysical position about things in the world, namely that things are 'undifferentiated, unstable and indeterminate' (this view has been labelled 'the indeterminacy thesis'). Pyrrho's indeterminacy thesis is not nihilism, but it is something remarkably close to it. Nietzsche too labelled Pyrrho as 'nihilist'.[52] He also called him 'a Buddhist for Greece'[53] thus anticipating, although with different motivations, the views of Christopher Beckwith, who has recently detailed a remarkably close correspondence between Pyrrho's statement about things being undifferentiated, unstable and indeterminate and a famous statement of the Buddha preserved in canonical texts.[54]

We cannot follow this lead any further at this point, but there seem to be some important connections between Pyrrho (as well as the nihilist/eliminativist tradition in ancient Greek metaphysics that includes Democritus and early atomists, Protagoras and the Cyrenaics too), early Buddhism and nihilism. These connections are still largely unexplored in the scholarship. What unexpected perspective could we gain if we looked at the second Buddha, Nāgārjuna, as a philosopher whose 'nihilist' views are understood not as the results of a sceptical strategy but as (hidden) philosophical beliefs about the world? What if behind the theory of emptiness that Nāgārjuna endorses there is really nihilism?[55] The answers to these questions and to those about Gorgias' actual commitment to nihilism are still in need of a fuller answer. I invite the reader to take the trend of arguments reconstructed this chapter as a first step in a new appraisal of ancient nihilism, both Greek and Buddhist.

4

On things. The origin and genealogy of Pyrrho's metaphysics

Pyrrho of Elis is, surprisingly, the most influential thinker nowadays among ancient Greek philosophers. While Plato, Aristotle and the other Hellenistic schools of the Stoics and the Epicureans are surely well accounted for as well as widely discussed in current scholarship, Pyrrho is very much present in contemporary debates, within and outside academia. Scepticism is an extremely lively approach in contemporary philosophy, taken up in different areas of analytic philosophy; it is inevitable that contemporary sceptics look at the founder of their tradition, Pyrrho, for inspiration and clarification. In addition to that, in the last decades Pyrrho has become a crucial figure also in the East/West philosophical interaction.

What I am going to do in this chapter is, once again, to return to the most troublesome, yet substantial source on Pyrrho, namely the Aristocles passage, to argue for a metaphysical reading of it (in contrast with other interpretations). The proposed interpretation is going to show that Pyrrho held a radical metaphysical thesis about things, that is, that they are undifferentiated, unstable and indeterminate. It is also going to be shown that Pyrrho's radical views are not fully novel in ancient Greek philosophy, since a close parallelism between Pyrrho's indeterminacy thesis and Protagoras' Secret Doctrine (as this is illustrated in the *Theaetetus*) is drawn, to show illuminating consonances between them. This parallelism does not exclude the fact that Pyrrho's views have also close analogies with similar doctrines held in early Buddhism (as recent studies have significantly shown). Instead of arguing for historical influence in way or another – something that would be extremely hard to assess, I shall claim that in his encounter with Indian philosophy Pyrrho is likely to have been the actual witness of a similarity of views between East and

West. These views are likely to have been first developed autonomously one from the other, to find later a common philosophical ground of interaction thanks to Pyrrho.

The Aristocles passage

Despite his huge influence on philosophers, both ancient and contemporary, it is difficult for us to reconstruct the philosophy of Pyrrho. As is known, he left nothing in writing. To reconstruct his thinking, we rely on very few sources, among which the so-called Aristocles passage stands for prominence. The passage is by the peripatetic philosopher Aristocles of Messene (most probably first century BC or early first century AD), who in his work *On Philosophy* criticizes the views of some Greek philosophers who preceded him and who, according to him, developed very un-Aristotelian views on knowledge in need to be refuted. Aristocles' passage reports the account of Pyrrho's thought as summarized by his most famous pupil, that is, Timon of Phlius. Aristocles' *On Philosophy*, however, is only summarized and preserved in the work of Eusebius, the fourth-century bishop of Caesarea. There is no full extant version of the work itself. We thus have an essential passage for constructing the thought of Pyrrho that is in fact a third-hand report: Eusebius on Aristocles on Timon (on Pyrrho). Yet, the passage has been seen as providing us with a reliable account of Pyrrho's views – and indeed it has been heavily relied on in current scholarship – exactly considering the highly detailed, even if compressed, account of Pyrrho's philosophy.[1] Here is a translation of the passage (Eusebius, PE 14.18.3–4=Chiesara F4=T53 Decleva Caizzi):

> It is necessary above all to consider our own knowledge; for if it is our nature to know nothing, there is no need to enquire any further into other things. There were some among the ancients, too, who made this statement, whom Aristotle has argued against. Pyrrho of Elis was also a strong advocate of this view. He himself has left nothing in writing; his pupil Timon, however, says that the person who aims to be happy must look to these three questions:
>
> 1. first, how are things by nature (*hopoîa péphuke tà prágmata*)?
> 2. second, in what way should we be disposed towards things (*tína chrē trópon hēmâs pròs autà diakeîsthai*)?

3. and finally, what will be the result for those who are so disposed (*tí periéstai toîs hoútōs échousi*)?
4. He [Timon] says that he [Pyrrho] says **1a)** that things are equally undifferentiated and unstable and indeterminate (*tà mèn oûn prágmatá phēsin apophaínein ep'ísēs tòn adiáphora kaì astáthmēta kaì anepíkrita*); **1b)** for this reason neither our sensations nor our opinions tell the truth or lie (*dià toûto mēte tàs aisthēseis hēmōn mēte tàs dóxas alētheúein ē pseúdesthai*). For this reason, then, **b1)** we should not trust them, but we should be without opinions, inclinations and wavering (*adoxástous kaì aklineîs kaì akradántous*), **b2)** saying about each single thing that it no more is than is not or both is and is not or neither is nor is not (*perí henòs hekástou légontas óti ou mâllon éstin ē ouk éstin ē kaì ésti kaì ouk éstin ē oute éstin oute ouk éstin*). Timon says that **c1)** the result for those who are disposed in this way will be first speechlessness (*aphasían*), but then imperturbability (*ataraxían*); and Aenesidemus says pleasure.

The nature of things

Aristocles' passage addresses three main questions: (1) first, what are things like by nature? (2) secondly, how should we dispose towards things; (3) thirdly, what will be the result for those who are correctly disposed towards things? One thing that the logic of the passage is clear about is that the three questions are closely interdependent. The answer to question (3) depends on the answer to question (2), which in turn depends on the answer to question (1). It is also clear that the passage gives us three definite answers to these questions, answers that we may claim are Pyrrho's authentic ones.[2]

What is being debated is the actual content of Pyrrho's answers, since the text itself is open to alternative interpretations, some of which are in stark contrast. Let us take Pyrrho's answer to the first question about the nature of things. Timon says that for Pyrrho things are equally '*adiáphora kaì astáthmēta kaì anepíkrita*'. These three adjectives can be translated as either 'undifferentiated and unstable and indeterminate' or as 'undifferentiable and unmeasurable and indeterminable'.[3] The Greek allows for both translations: while the first, which has here been adopted, makes *things* (*tà prágmatá*) in themselves as being undifferentiated, unstable and indeterminate, the second translation shifts the emphasis from things in themselves to perceiving subjects, making human beings (as such) incapable to determine, measure or differentiate things. The first translation thus makes Pyrrho's answer a metaphysical answer about how things really are, that is, intrinsically undifferentiated, unstable and indeterminate. Alternatively, the second translation makes Pyrrho's answer an epistemological one, while claiming that it depends on us if things are (seen as) undifferentiable and unmeasurable and indeterminable. That is, it is because of our epistemological inabilities that things are undifferentiable and unmeasurable and indeterminable.

Both the metaphysical and the epistemological interpretations have their own strong advocates; this is not the right place to overview the pros and cons of each interpretation.[4] On my account, there are stronger reasons to adopt the metaphysical reading over the epistemological one and I shall proceed by explaining some of these reasons.[5] As we have seen Aristocles' passage is centred on a strictly consequential logic so that the answer to each of the questions entails the answer to the previous one. After the claim about things being *adiáphora* and *astáthmēta* and *anepíkrita*, the next deductive step in the passage is this one: 'for this reason neither our sensations nor our opinions tell the truth or lie'. While Pyrrho's first reported answer allows for some ambiguity in the translation, this second sentence about sensations and opinions has no ambiguity. So, either we have (1) that things are undifferentiated, unstable and indeterminate (metaphysical reading) and for this reason neither our sensations nor our opinions tell the truth or lie or (2) things are undifferentiable, unmeasurable, indeterminable (epistemological reading) and for this reason neither our sensations nor our opinions tell the truth or lie. But the latter alternative hardly makes sense. If we cannot discover the nature of things because we are epistemologically incapacitated to do that, well, we shall be in the position *not* to tell anything about our sensations and opinions. For us to say anything about the truth-value of our sensations and opinions, we must be able to say what the things these opinions are about are like – something that is openly denied by the preceding (epistemological) claim that things are undifferentiable, unmeasurable and indeterminable.[6]

On the contrary, it does make good sense to say, on (1), that that things are undifferentiated, unstable and indeterminate (metaphysical reading) and for this reason neither our sensations nor our opinions tell the truth or lie. It is exactly because things in the material world are intrinsically undifferentiated, unstable and indeterminate that our opinions and sensations are neither true nor false. For this to be the case, our opinions and sensations should either manage or fail to grasp how things actually are – but this is impossible, given the previous metaphysical claim about things being undifferentiated, unstable and indeterminate. It is really the case that if things are undifferentiated, unstable and indeterminate, our opinions and sensations cannot either tell the truth or lie (about them).

The metaphysical interpretation makes good sense of the transmitted text, while the epistemological reading seems to fail to do so. For this reason, some proposers of the epistemological reading suggest some emendations to the transmitted text to be put in place, so to read: 'on the account of the fact that (replacing the original Greek "*dià toūto*: for this reason" with "*dià tó*: on the account of the fact that") our opinions and sensations cannot either tell the truth or lie'.[7] If the emendation is adopted, the assertion about things being *adiáphora* and *astáthmēta* and *anepíkrita* becomes a consequence of the assertion about opinions and sensations being deprived of any truth-values, not a reason for it to be true. The textual and philological reasons behind this emendation are weak – as Bett has shown.[8] Not only is this the case, but also and more perspicuously the emended text would read in this way: 'things are undifferentiable, unmeasurable and indeterminable on the account of the fact that neither our sensations nor our opinions tell the truth or lie'. Again, this makes little sense. If we claim that neither our sensations nor our opinions tell the truth or lie, this will presuppose that we have discovered the true nature of things so that we are in the condition of saying something about the truth-value of our opinions and sensations (about things); so, things *could not be* undifferentiable, unmeasurable and indeterminable. To conclude then, the proposed emendation is not only philologically weak but also philosophically, since it makes the text hardly intelligible.[9]

The metaphysical reading has thus some strength that commends it over the epistemological one. It also makes excellent sense of the transmitted text as well as advancing coherently a philosophical view that is both radical and, it seems at least prima facie, unprecedented in the history of Greek thought: things are ontologically undifferentiated, unstable and indeterminate in such a way that our opinions and sensations neither tell the truth nor lie (about things). What we need to look at now is the approach one should take towards things if these are intrinsically indeterminate.

Our disposition towards things

Timon's report as transmitted by Aristocles goes on by saying that 'for this reason, then, we should not trust them (i.e., our sensations and opinions), but we should be without opinions, inclinations and wavering (*adoxástous kaì aklineîs kaì akradántous*),[10] saying about each single thing that it no more is, than is not, or both is and is not, or neither is nor is not (*perí henòs hekástou légontas óti ou mâllon éstin ē ouk éstin ē kaì ésti kaì ouk éstin ē oute éstin oute ouk éstin)*'. The second part of Aristocles' passage reports Pyrrho's answer to the second question – how we should be disposed towards things once we have understood that they are *adiáphora* and *astáthmēta* and *anepíkrita*.

Again, Pyrrho's answer does fit well with the metaphysical reading previously illustrated. Since things are intrinsically indeterminate and our opinions neither tell the truth nor lie, we should be without opinions, since they lack any truth-values – they can be neither true nor false. In addition to having no opinions, we should also be without any inclinations towards accepting or rejecting them, since they do not say anything definite about things in the world. Finally, we should not only be without opinions and inclinations but also without wavering about opinions (about things), so that we do not oscillate between one opinion (about one thing) and the opposite one (about the same thing), or between having and not any opinion at all. It is clear enough that the highly original approach to our opinions about things Pyrrho is reported to have adopted grows out from the radical view about them that is expressed in the metaphysical reading of the first part: the suggested disposition described in the second part of the passage does fit nicely with the metaphysical outlook implicit in the first. This is also confirmed by the way the second part ends. That is, it concludes by suggesting that we should say 'about each single thing that it no more is, than is not, or both is and is not, or neither is nor is not'. This is, again, a metaphysical suggestion, which has little to do with the suspension of judgement that is later associated with the expression 'no more' and later scepticism.[11]

The 'no more' slogan as it is spelt in the Aristocles' passage does push us to say something about things and is thus a metaphysical invitation – the only trouble is that it is, again, a very peculiar way to say something about things. The text again allows for two possible translations/interpretations. I give the original Greek once again: *perí henòs hekástou légontas óti ou mâllon éstin ē ouk éstin ē kaì ésti kaì ouk éstin ē oute éstin oute ouk éstin*. While following Pyrrho's advice to be without opinions, inclinations and wavering, we have two options:[12]

1) that for each thing no more is than is not
   or that it both is and is not
   or that it neither is nor is not.
2) that for each thing that it no more
   is
   than is not
   or both is and is not
   neither is nor is not.

On option (1), we have a trilemma, on option (2) we have a tetralemma. There has been a long debate on how to read this ambiguous passage. Reale and Decleva Caizzi incline for option (1) and argue that Pyrrho is here literally rejecting what Aristotle says at *Metaphysics* 4.1008a30–34 (namely the argument against those who say neither yes or no, but yes and no, and again deny both options, eventually saying neither yes nor no). In short, both Reale and Decleva Caizzi take Pyrrho here as denying the principle of non-contradiction.[13]

With some good reasons Bett has suggested that to take Pyrrho's words as a trilemma, while syntactically possible, does not fit well with the overall logic of the text.[14] If we adopt the first reading (the trilemma), Pyrrho is in fact taken to suggest that for each thing we are in the condition to choose between one of three viable options, namely that something is both F and not-F, neither F nor not-F, or F no more than not-F. But it is difficult to see how this could be the case, given the preceding argument that, since things are intrinsically indeterminate, we should not trust our opinions about them: our beliefs neither tell the truth nor lie. If we affirm one of the three viable options about things that are available on the trilemma, we should contravene the explicit claim not to rely on our opinions.[15]

It does seem therefore that the trilemma, while being a possible translation of the transmitted text, does not fit the philosophical argument that Pyrrho is reported to be making in the Aristocles passage. On the contrary, the tetralemma makes good sense, philosophically, and is in perfect accordance with the preceding arguments: about things being *adiáphora* and *astáthmēta* and *anepíkrita;* about opinions lacking any truth-values; about us being without opinions, wavering and inclinations. The tetralemma in fact says that for each thing we have four possibilities: either that it is F, or not-F, both F and not-F, neither F nor not-F. Contrary to what the trilemma does, the four possibilities that are explicitly illustrated in the tetralemma exhaust the logical space of all possibilities for one thing to be something. If we adopt the tetralemma as a suitable way to speak about things, we shall be in the condition neither to affirm nor to deny any of the four possibilities that are on offer. If we affirm or deny any of them, we shall automatically be contradicting one of the other three possibilities about things that are available; and this would be a logically invalid step to take if we aim for consistency. So, the only option that we seem to have is neither to deny nor affirm any of the four possibilities that are recommended in the tetralemma and that are the only four possibilities we have to say something *definite* about things.[16]

With this we now go back to Pyrrho's first statement about things being *adiáphora* and *astáthmēta* and *anepíkrita*. The actual rejection of the four possibilities that are explicitly illustrated in the tetralemma is the only option we have, to avoid saying something *definite* or *determinate* about things. While saying that each thing no more is, than is not, or both is and is not, or neither is nor is not, we are not committed to any of the four viable options. The tetralemma is also the only possible way that is available to us for not relying on our opinions: while we neither affirm nor deny all the four possibilities that are available in the tetralemma, we show that we have indeed no opinions.

The outcome for those who understand the very nature of things

The first two questions that Timon's Pyrrho says need to be asked, namely how things are by nature and how we should be disposed towards them (once we understand how things are by nature) have now been answered. On the metaphysical reading that I have been recommending, for Pyrrho things are undifferentiated, unstable and indeterminate; for this reason, we should not trust our opinions, since they can say anything neither true nor false about the way things are. For this reason, again, we must be without opinions, inclinations and wavering about things saying that each thing no more is, than is not, or that both is and is not, or that neither is nor is not.

What shall we gain if we understand the true nature of things and become aware of the epistemological unreliability of our opinions about things? This is the last question that needs asking and the answer Pyrrho is supposed to have given is the following one:

> The result for those who are so disposed will be first speechlessness, but then freedom from worry (*prōton mèn aphasian, epeita d'ataraxían*), and Aenesidemus says pleasure.

This is, once again, a very radical outcome for those who have understood Pyrrho's previous claims. The focus on the present chapter is not on this aspect of Aristocles' passage, yet it is important to spend few words on why speechlessness and imperturbability are the main result for those who are correctly disposed towards things. Once we come to understand that things lack any ontological determination; that our opinions can say nothing about the way things are; that the tetralemma is the only way we can something meaningful about things but that for its own nature the tetralemma is also a way to say nothing definite about things; after realizing all this, we may come to understand that the best way forward is to stay silent – to say nothing at all. This speechlessness may well derive from a sort of initial puzzlement about realizing the indeterminacy of things as well as from the fact that our opinions are wholly unusable.[17] Yet, after this initial puzzlement that leads us to silence, we may start to feel the sort of imperturbability that comes with realizing that things are utterly indeterminate and that our opinions about them have no epistemological consistency whatsoever.[18]

As shown in the preceding sections, there are good reasons to take the Aristocles passage as providing us with Pyrrho's metaphysical view that *tà prágmatá* are *adiáphora kaì astáthmēta kaì anepíkrita*, that is: things are undifferentiated, unstable and indeterminate. We have seen that, at least on the reading I recommend, this metaphysical view explains all the other views, both epistemological and practical, which are discussed in the Aristocles passage. Our focus now is on the radical view about things that Pyrrho is made to argue for, for it is not easy to understand its full significance and meaning. What does it really mean to say that things are undifferentiated, unstable and indeterminate? Since this is not immediately obvious, it would be wise to try to figure out the philosophical climate in which Pyrrho matured his metaphysical thesis.

Until recently, Pyrrho's views as expounded in the Aristocles passage have been tentatively explained in relation to other doctrines held by other Greek philosophers, as well as in the more general context of ancient Greek thought. This attempt, however, has not been too successful, since Pyrrho's metaphysical view is usually seen as a novelty in Greek philosophy, with very few passages or authors anticipating it. If we look at the most thorough and systematic account of Pyrrho's indeterminacy thesis (as he labels it), that is, the one developed by Richard Bett in Bett (2000), few similarities are drawn between Pyrrho and his predecessors. While the linkage between Pyrrho's ethics of imperturbability and Democritus has been highlighted more than once,[19] Pyrrho's metaphysical view about reality as this has been reconstructed on the basis of the Aristocles passage has been understood as having very few antecedents in ancient Greek philosophy. Bett recognizes a fairly widespread tendency in thinkers after and before Socrates to take perceptual reality as inherently variable.[20] The discussion that Aristotle images to have with the deniers of the principle of non-contradiction in *Metaphysics Gamma* reflects the import of such a tendency in pre-Socratic and Socratic philosophy.[21] Yet, Bett argues, except for a possible linkage with a view held by Anaxarchus of Abdera, the atomist thinker who travelled to India with Pyrrho,[22] the only two places where Pyrrho's indeterminacy thesis have a clear antecedent are two passages of Plato, one in the *Republic* and the other in the *Theaetetus*.[23]

The most significant is the one in the *Theaetetus*. At the end of the Protagorean section of that dialogue, while discussing the Heraclitean view that all things are in flux, Socrates remarks: 'What has really emerged is that, if all things are in motion, every answer, on whatever subject, is equally correct, both "it is thus" and "it is not thus"' (183a2–6). Socrates further highlights that 'one must not use even the word "thus"; for this "thus" would be no longer in motion; nor yet "not thus" for here again there is no motion. The exponents of this theory need to establish some other language; as it is, they have no words that are consistent with their hypothesis – unless it would perhaps suit them best to use "not at all thus" in a quite indefinite sense' (183b1–5). What Socrates says here with reference to the Heracliteans (as their theory is being reconstructed in the *Theaetetus* at least) does seem remarkably close to the way Pyrrho says we should talk about things in the Aristocles passage: 'about each single thing [it is to be said] that it no more is, than is not, or both is and is not, or neither is nor is not'.

There is therefore at least one obvious precedent of Pyrrho's indeterminacy thesis clearly stated in Plato. What to say about possible non-Greek influences on Pyrrho? Here the obvious candidate is Indian Buddhist philosophy. Bett rejects any substantial influence on the philosophy of Pyrrho on the part of the Indian philosophers, highlighting a possible sharing of similar 'life-style and broad philosophical attitude' (Bett 2000, p. 178).[24] Bett's claims have been, however, recently challenged by two important works on Pyrrho and Buddhism that have in diverse ways highlighted close analogies between Pyrrho's views and early Buddhism. To these works we now turn.

Pyrrho in India: Beckwith and Kuzminski

Two recent books have aimed to explain Pyrrho's views in the context of Buddhist thought. In a bold and thought-provoking monograph, *Greek Buddha. Pyrrho's encounter with Early Buddhism in Central Asia* (Princeton University Press 2015), Christopher Beckwith advances a variety of revolutionary claims about Pyrrho's philosophy. It is known that Pyrrho travelled to India with Alexander the Great; he is reported to have spent a considerable time in Western India, where he is said to have come into close contact with Indian philosophy.[25] Diogenes Laertius openly writes that after having encountered Indian philosophers, Pyrrho's developed 'his most noble philosophy' (DL 9.61). Although the historical record of Pyrrho's trip to India is foggy, it is highly likely that the protracted permanence of Pyrrho in India and his contacts with Indian philosophers influenced his philosophical outlook. By relying on a mix of historical facts and philosophical arguments, Beckwith claims that while leaving Greece as a painter interested in philosophy, Pyrrho became a real philosopher in India and developed his views *only* when he encountered

Indian philosophers. To make his point, Beckwith highlights a close textual parallelism between the views ascribed to Pyrrho in the Aristocles passage and some other views that are at the core of early Buddhism. Beckwith provides the following translation of the Aristocles passage:

> As for pragmata 'matters, questions, topics', they are all *adiaphora* 'undifferentiated by a logical differentia', and *astathmēta* 'unstable, unbalanced, not measurable' and *anepikrita* 'unjudged, unfixed, undecidable'. Therefore, neither our sense-perceptions nor our 'views, theories, beliefs' (*doxai*) tell us the truth or lie [about *pragmata*]; so we certainly should not rely on them [to do it]. Rather, we should be *adoxastous* 'without views', *aklineis* 'uninclined' [toward this side or that], and *akradantous* 'unwavering [in our refusal to choose]', saying about every single one that it no more is than is not or it both is and is not or it neither is nor is not.[26]

As we can see from the translation provided, Beckwith accepts the traditional logical pattern that from the first metaphysical answer about the nature of things moves to the epistemological consequences of that answer, to end with the practical results to be gained by someone who knows the true nature of things. In doing so, Beckwith seems to reject the epistemological reading of the Aristocles passage, while endorsing a peculiar metaphysical interpretation of it. He argues in fact for '*pragmata*' (to be undifferentiated, unstable and indeterminate) to refer not to 'things or events in the material world' (as the metaphysical reading provided in the previous section does) but to 'ethical matters'. In this way Pyrrho is seen as providing a metaphysical claim that has, however, an ethical implication.[27]

It is at this point that Beckwith presses for a close parallelism between Pyrrho and early Buddhism. He argues that the list of the three Greek adjectives as referred to *pragmata* in the Aristocles passage, that is, *adiáphora*, *astáthmēta* and *anepíkrita*, 'corresponds closely to a famous statement of the Buddha preserved in canonical texts' (Beckwith 2015, p. 28). The statement Beckwith refers to is known as the *Trilaksana*, the 'Three Characteristics' and goes like this:

> All dharmas are *anitya* 'impermanent' … All dharmas are *duhkha* 'unsatisfactory, imperfect, unstable' … All dharmas are *anātman* 'without an innate self-identity'. (Beckwith 2015, p. 29)[28]

As we have seen in Chapter 2, in Buddhist thought *dharmas* are the basic constituents of reality. Beckwith makes a compelling case to show that in both the Aristocles passage and in the *Trilaksana*, (ethical) matters are said to be lacking all ontological determinations. Beckwith argues for Pyrrho to be the Greek Buddha exactly in light of the close analogies between Pyrrho's thought as this emerges from the Aristocles passage (and from other ancient sources too) and early Buddhism. He also makes the bold case that the Aristocles passage may be read as the first evidence on early Buddhism, an oral tradition that was not crystallized at the time of Pyrrho's travel to India and whose main written sources are much later in time.[29] Beckwith does make a fascinating case for Pyrrho's philosophy as deeply connected to Buddhism, thus explaining all the main features of that philosophy as the result of Pyrrho's encounter with Indian philosophy. In this way because of the metaphysical views that he develops ('[views that are] completely unprecedented and unparalleled in Greek thought': p. 28), Pyrrho is made to appear alien to ancient Greek philosophy as a whole.[30]

As far as the Pyrrho-Buddhism linkage is concerned, Beckwith's claims have been partly resisted, among others, by Adrian Kuzminski in his 2021 book, *Pyrrhonian Buddhism* (Rouledge).[31] In his study, Kuzminski shows how Pyrrhonism cannot be explained in the context of ancient Greek philosophy only. He singles out Democritus as the only philosopher who may have deeply influenced Pyrrho. Yet, he remarks, Democritus' atomism alone cannot explain Pyrrhonism as the kind of metaphysical and epistemological doctrine that it is. Pyrrho, Kuzminski continues, was an original thinker who transformed the metaphysical claim of Democritus' atomism into a new, original doctrine, thanks to his (Pyrrho's) encounter with early Buddhism in his trip to India.

Democritus' atomism is a view of reality and matter that makes atoms the physical, ultimate elements of reality. On the other hand, Buddhism, as Pyrrho may have encountered it, shows that everything is a transient phenomenon with no ontological as well as temporal durability. By means of an original combination with Buddhism, Kuzminski claims, Pyrrho developed Greek atomism into a phenomenalistic doctrine, which as such has no real antecedent in Greek thought. Kuzminski writes:

The question is not whether Pyrrhonism is essentially a Greek or Indian philosophy. The question is whether Greek and Indian philosophies could actually overlap or even merge, whether aspects of each could find a smooth and harmonious integration with aspects of the other so as to produce a seamless whole. I propose to consider that this is exactly what may have occurred, that Pyrrho's achievement was precisely the creation of such a synthesis – an atomism derived from Democritus with a phenomenalism derived from Buddhism – which we can call Pyrrhonian Buddhism. (p. 18)

He goes on to say:

To understand the emergence of phenomenalistic atomism, I suggest that we imagine Pyrrho bringing to India the mind-set of a Democritean atomist, and then imagine him radically transforming the dogmatically postulated, imperceptible atomism of Democritus by recognizing as atoms the phenomenal, perceptible elements of experience found in the Buddhist doctrine of dependent origination. In making this move, Pyrrho, in effect, replaced the abstract conceptual atomism of the Democriteans with the experiential phenomenalism of the Buddhists.[32]

Pyrrho and Protagoras' Secret Doctrine

Against rival understanding, in this chapter a metaphysical reading of Pyrrho's philosophy has been argued for, one that is legitimated by a plausible interpretation of the Aristocles passage. Although spelt differently and with different emphasis, the metaphysical reading is endorsed by scholars taking radically alternative approach as far as the origins of Pyrrho's views is concerned. Bett reads Pyrrho's philosophical enterprise as mainly deriving its inspiration and impetus from only within Greek philosophy. On the contrary, Beckwith takes Pyrrho's metaphysical doctrine as wholly explicable in the context of Buddhist thought and as something eminently alien to the Greek spirit. Lastly, Kuzminski takes a middle way between these two approaches, suggesting that while deriving from Democritean atomism, Pyrrho's metaphysical outlook is an original combination of that atomism with Buddhist phenomenalism.[33]

What I aim to do in the last sections of this chapter is to ground more firmly Pyrrho's indeterminacy thesis into ancient Greek philosophy, while also (partly) endorsing the attempts of those scholars such as Beckwith and Kuzminski who see remarkably close resemblances between Pyrrho's metaphysical views and some other Buddhist views. As for the genealogy of Pyrrho's thought, however, I claim that it is neither fully explicable within the context of ancient Greek philosophy (as Bett says), nor in the context of early Buddhist thought only (as Beckwith claims), nor as an original combination of ancient Greek and Buddhist views (as Kuzminski argues for). What I claim is that Pyrrho's indeterminacy thesis has a clear antecedent in a lengthy section of Plato's *Theaetetus* that has so far not been read against Pyrrho's indeterminacy thesis.[34] This linkage makes Pyrrho as the original elaborator, perhaps the final 'systematiser' of a metaphysical view that had already had some (wide) circulation in ancient Greek philosophy before him. At the same time, I reckon that the philosophical affinity between Pyrrho's indeterminacy thesis and some Buddhist views is indeed there for us to appreciate. More than a matter of influence in one direction or another, which is something extremely hard to assess, it seems to me that the affinity between Pyrrho's metaphysical views and Buddhist doctrines witnesses the fact that two different philosophical traditions may have developed similar views, independently of one from the other.

We have seen that Bett argues for Pyrrho's indeterminacy thesis to be anticipated in a passage of Plato's *Theaetetus* where it is said that since they think that all things are in flux, the Heracliteans should say that 'one must not use even the word "thus"; for this "thus" would be no longer in motion; nor yet "not thus" for here again there is no motion. The exponents of this theory need to establish some other language; as it is, they have no words that are consistent with their hypothesis – unless it would perhaps suit them best to use "not at all thus" in a quite indefinite sense' (183b1–5). Yet, what Socrate says here with reference to the Heracliteans is the final upshot of a much-detailed argument that has previously received much attention on the part of Socrates and Theaetetus, that is, Protagoras' Secret Doctrine.[35] It is Socrates himself that makes the connection between the two sections of the *Theatetus*, when he says: 'You will remember, perhaps, that we said in the earlier stage of the argument that there is nothing which in itself is just one thing (i.e., Protagoras' Secret Doctrine: at *Tht.* 152a8 ff); and that this applies to the active and passive factors (i.e., the fundamental elements of the two accounts of perception developed out of the Secret Doctrine). It is by the association of the two with one another that they generate perceptions and the things perceived; and in so doing, the active factor becomes such and such, while the passive factor becomes percipient' (182b1–6).

It is exactly because of these views that we should use the expressions Socrates refers to at *Tht* 183b1–5 about things being 'thus', 'not thus' and 'not at all thus' and so on, which very closely reminds us of Pyrrho's formula in the Aristocles passage. What are the main features, then, of Protagoras' Secret Doctrine? As shown in Chapters 1 and 2, Protagoras' Secret Doctrine is a quite elaborate theory. Its core are two interrelated metaphysical theses about indeterminacy, which have a semantic consequence: the ineffability of things and of the properties we usually attach to things. The origin of indeterminacy is flux. Things cannot be determinate entities and cannot have determinate properties because everything is in flux. Nothing is because everything is coming to be. Socrates carries on by developing a two-stage account of perception arising from Protagoras' Secret Doctrine. The final outcome of this account is that neither (perceived) objects nor (perceiving) subjects have any ontological consistency on their own, because they both arise as that very object and that very subject only in the context of a temporary encounter that happens during perception. The ontological identity of both objects and subjects is ontologically unstable, since everything keeps flowing and changing all the time and in all respects. Indeed, and strictly speaking, there are neither actual objects nor real subjects in the perceptual process. Because of the absence of ontological determinacy, we are caught in the trap of semantic ineffability: we cannot name material things because there is, properly speaking, nothing there to be named.[36]

The metaphysical account that Protagoras' Secret Doctrine advances is remarkably original and similar to the one Pyrrho is made to argue for when he says that things are *adiáphora* and *astáthmēta* and *anepíkrita*, that is, undifferentiated, unstable, indeterminate. Indeed, the three adjectives denoting Pyrrho's conception of things can also be applied to material things in Protagoras' Secret Doctrine. I have already highlighted that the central view of Protagoras' Secret Doctrine is that nothing is one thing. This view can be read as a profession of metaphysical indeterminacy about things.[37] At the same time, in the context of Protagoras' Secret Doctrine where flux plays a vital role, things can well be said as being unstable, since '*astathmēta*' does refer to things as being unbalanced, dragged upon here and there because of their intrinsic ontological instability. Lastly, in the metaphysical picture painted by Protagoras' Secret Doctrine, things are indeed *adiáphora* because there is no ontological difference in the metaphysical substratum of the world, which is all devoid of ontologically determinate items (there seems to be neither objects nor subjects in account of the material world as depicted by Protagoras' Secret Doctrine).

Not only is there a strict parallelism between Pyrrho's metaphysical views as these are reported in the Aristocles passage and Protagoras' Secret Doctrine; the ineffability that seems to arise almost naturally for someone adopting Protagoras' views is something remarkably close to the kind of speechlessness that in the Aristocles passage is one of the final outcomes for someone holding Pyrrho's views. Both the Heracliteans and those sharing Pyrrho's metaphysics should stay silent if they sticked to our traditional language, which is not apt for capturing the manifest indeterminacy of things in the world. From an epistemological point of view, Protagoras' relativism and Pyrrho's scepticism do differ, so there is no common approach to the role of perceptions and beliefs in their respective philosophies; yet the metaphysical background on which their different epistemologies rely on is astonishingly similar and is one rooted in ontological indeterminacy, instability and lack of differentiation of and between things.

Conclusion

While providing a plausible reading of the Aristocles passage, in this chapter it has been argued that Pyrrho held a metaphysical thesis that took things in the world to be undifferentiated, unstable and indeterminate. Despite its original radicality, it has also been claimed that Pyrrho's indeterminacy thesis had had some circulation in ancient Greek philosophy before him. Protagoras' Secrete Doctrine in the *Theaetetus* shows itself to have striking similarities with Pyrrho's metaphysics of indeterminacy. This makes Pyrrho likely to have taken inspiration for his metaphysical outlook in the context of ancient Greek philosophy, which was a fertile soil for such an outlook to be adopted.

Yet, as shown in diverse ways in recent comparative studies, there are remarkably close analogies between Pyrrho's (metaphysical) views and early Buddhism. For early (and later) Buddhism the three hallmarks of all phenomenal existence are impermanence (*anitya*), unsteadiness (*duhkha*), lack of determination (*anātman*). These features apply to all *dharmas* conceived of as the primary elements of existence. These features of *dharmas*, which are illustrated in the *Three Characteristics,* a canonical text in Buddhism, are mirrored in three adjectives that are prominent in the Aristocles passage and that tell us how things are by nature for Pyrrho: *adiáphora, astáthmēta, anepíkrita*. This parallelism reveals an analogy of metaphysical views between Pyrrho and early Buddhism that is there for us to appreciate. The analogy between Greek and Indian metaphysics is strengthened even more when we take in due account the fact that, as just shown in the chapter, the three adjectives describing Pyrrho's metaphysical outlook can also be applied to the views that constitute the backbone of Protagoras' Secret Doctrine in the *Theaeteteus*. In this way, one can well argue that, for the transitive property, some central tenets about reality that are typical of Buddhism are indeed reflected in an important section of the *Theaetetus*.

What these parallelisms and analogies demonstrate is that the similarity of metaphysical views between Greek philosophy (Pyrrho and Protagoras' Secret Doctrine) and early Buddhism is indeed strong. On the basis of these parallelisms and analogies, one may argue that Pyrrho is likely to have ventured to India already philosophically prepared for his radical view of reality, just to discover that the same view was adopted by other thinkers such as the early Buddhists. He may well have refined further his metaphysical doctrine after having met Buddhist philosophers in India, but the view was already there in his philosophical outlook. This convergence of views between Greek and Buddhist philosophies is thus not a matter of influence in way or another; more perspicuously, it looks as if separate discoveries of the same metaphysical view converged in Pyrrho, who acted as the physical *trait d'union* between the two philosophical worlds.[38]

5

The Cyrenaics on indeterminacy

The Cyrenaics

After having met in the previous chapters Protagoras and Vasubandhu, Gorgias and Nāgārjuna, and Pyrrho, it is now time to deal with the Cyrenaics. As briefly mentioned in the Introduction, the Cyrenaics are a Socratic school that lasted through Hellenism. His supposed founder, Aristippus from Cyrene, was a contemporary and associate of Socrates. Through his daughter Arete and his grandson Aristippus the Younger, the school developed a lasting legacy that was defended and reinvented by the later sects of the school, whose main figures were Hegesias the Death Persuader, Anniceris and Theodorus the Godless.[1]

While the next chapter is devoted to discussing the centrality of the subject in Cyrenaic philosophy by dealing with solipsism and privacy, in this chapter I put forward an interpretation of the Cyrenaics as ultimately committed to metaphysical indeterminacy. In doing so, I expand an unconventional interpretation that I first developed in *The Cyrenaics* (Acumen 2012) more than ten years ago. While my metaphysical reading has surely helped to assess Cyrenaic philosophy under a new light, it remains true that some scholars have criticised and opposed it. In this chapter, I make a fresher case for the Cyrenaics as being indeterminists in metaphysics by also answering, mainly in the footnotes, the criticism that has been levelled against my interpretation by Richard Bett and, mainly, by Tim O'Keefe.[2]

According to the sceptical interpretation, the Cyrenaics defended a kind of strict subjectivism with regard to our own private affections and, at the same time, discharged as hopeless the possibility that we may come to know what causes them.[3] A crucial passage by Sextus Empiricus is usually taken to show the point:

The Cyrenaics hold that affections [*pathē*] are the criteria [of truth] and that they alone are apprehended and are infallible [*kai mona katalambanesthai kai adiapseusta tunchanein*]. None of the things that have caused the affections [*tōn de pepoiēkotōn ta pathē*] is, on the contrary, apprehensible or infallible. They say that it is possible to state infallibly and truly and firmly and incorrigibly that we are being whitened or sweetened [*oti men gar leuikanometha, phasi, kai glukazometha, dunaton legein adiapseustōs kai bebaiōs kai alēthōs kai anexelenktōs*]. It is not possible however to say that the thing productive of our affection [*to empoiētikon tou pathous*] is white or sweet, because one may be disposed whitely even by something that is not-white or may be sweetened by something that is not-sweet. (*M.* VII 191–2=*SSR* IV A 213).[4]

In the passage, Sextus reports the kernel of Cyrenaic subjectivism: for the Cyrenaics we may truly and infallibly affirm that we have an affection of white but we cannot say that what we perceive as white is white in itself. Things in the world – 'things that have caused the affections' – are not apprehensible or infallible, while our affections are such that we cannot be mistaken about them. The contrast here is, the sceptical interpretation goes, between *infallible affections* and *unknowable items* in the world (causing affections in us). The contrast is traditionally sceptic: we know how things appear to us, but not how things are in themselves.[5] The Cyrenaics took this contrast and stretched it at a full extent by coining neologisms such as 'to be whitened, sweetened', to express the full epistemological privacy of our affections. In adopting such a position, like other sceptics, the Cyrenaics cannot be credited with any interest in metaphysics, since they openly profess things in the world to be unknowable.

The sceptical reading of the Cyrenaics I have just summarily reconstructed is at the root of the interpretation I wish to resist. I will now construct the best case I can to show that a rival interpretation of Cyrenaic philosophy is available. According to this rival interpretation, the Cyrenaics may have had metaphysical commitments that went parallel to their epistemological subjectivism and that would explain some features of their philosophy in a more convincing way.

The alternative interpretation

Let us begin with a preliminary remark about the Cyrenaics' attitude towards metaphysics. In this connection, Sextus reports the following view:

> The Cyrenaics appear to confine themselves to ethics only, and to dismiss physics and logic as contributing nothing to the happiness of our life. Some, however, have suggested that this view about them is actually refuted by the very fact that the Cyrenaics divided ethics into sub-branches: one, having to do with what has to be done or avoided; another dealing with affections; a third one on actions; the fourth concerned with causes; and a final one dealing with arguments. (*M.* VII 11=*SSR* IV A 168; see also Sen. *Ep. ad. Lucilium* XIV 1, 12=*SSR* IV A 165)

The passage seems to lend support to the sceptical interpretation of the Cyrenaics in so far as it begins with a rather peremptory statement about the exclusive interest in ethics the Cyrenaics appear to have had. According to one possible reading of the passage, for the Cyrenaics no metaphysics and no other branch of philosophy apart from ethics will be ever contributing to the happiness of life. Yet, the support that the passage may offer to the sceptical interpretation is only apparent. If properly understood, in fact, it offers arguments *against* that interpretation. The passage insists that the Cyrenaics had wide interests for every branch of philosophy, since ethics was further divided by them in sub-branches that correspond roughly to ethics proper, epistemology, theory of action, metaphysics and logic. This passage, therefore, confirms that the Cyrenaics had interest also for epistemology and metaphysics, not only for ethics.

This is one first difficulty for the sceptical interpretation: how could any interest of the Cyrenaics for metaphysics be explained if they believed metaphysical knowledge to be wholly unattainable? It seems that the sceptical interpretation has close analogies with old-fashioned readings of the Cyrenaics, when Aristippus' followers were understood as ultra-hedonists, with no other proper philosophical views to defend, not even the original epistemology on which scholars have focused more recently. Research in recent decades has amply shown how systematic and wide-ranging Cyrenaic philosophy as a whole was. As the quoted passage suggests, metaphysics is among the philosophical interests the Cyrenaics had. It is exactly such a wide-ranging spectrum of philosophical interests that helps explaining the relevance and importance of the Cyrenaics both in the context of ancient thought and also for us today.

The sceptical exegete of the Cyrenaics may well insist that Sextus openly says that 'none of the things that have caused the affections [*tōn de pepoiēkotōn ta pathē*] is, on the contrary, apprehensible (*mēden katalēpton*) or infallible'. Sextus reports the same view when he distinguishes the Cyrenaics from the Sceptics in *PH* 215: '[The sceptics] suspend judgement – as far as the argument goes – about external things, while the Cyrenaics assert that they have an inapprehensible (*akatalēpton*) nature.' The term Sextus uses in both passages is the canonical term '*katalpêton*', which the sceptics usually employ to express the epistemological apprehensibility of things.[6]

Now, what could it mean that, in contrast with infallible affections, things are inapprehensible? I see two possible explanations: either that we are epistemologically incapable to arrive at the very nature of things for a variety of reasons, such as those that the ancient sceptics have usually brought to attention with their modes of suspending judgement; or, alternatively, things are inapprehensible because *by their own nature* they are not knowable, that is, there is nothing determinate there to be known for us. The sceptical exegete of the Cyrenaics takes them to be committed to the first explanation: the Cyrenaics claim that only our affections are apprehensible exactly because they are aware that we cannot grasp the ontological features of the things that cause affections in us. I will defend the second explanation: the Cyrenaics claim that we know our affections and not the very things in the world because the latter are metaphysically indeterminate. Even more radically, I will try to show that the Cyrenaics may have ventured to stretch their metaphysical views to the point where material things are denied to be existing.

In other words, what I suggest is that the Cyrenaics endorsed a metaphysics of indeterminacy, which I also take to be working at the root of their epistemological subjectivism. On the basis of this interpretation, the Cyrenaics declare the exclusive apprehensibility of our affections because there is widespread indeterminacy in the world and there are no determinate objects there to be apprehended for us. On this understanding, we can simply know how things appear to us, not how they really are, because material things are metaphysically indeterminate.

Metaphysical indeterminacy

From a purely philosophical standpoint, is the claim that things are inapprehensible because ultimately indeterminate a plausible one? What does it mean to say that things are indeterminate? In her critical survey of antecedents of scepticism in early Greek philosophy, Mitzi Lee insists that some predecessors of ancient scepticism conceived of things as inapprehensible for ontological reasons (among those predecessors, however, she does not include the Cyrenaics), such reasons being the following ones: contradictionism (the view that everything is both F and not-F), flux (the view that everything is always changing from F to not-F) and indeterminacy (the view that nothing is anymore F or is determinately F to any greater extent that it is not-F). She rightly remarks: 'If then all of nature is fundamentally indeterminate, and nothing that exists has a definite nature, then it will be impossible to say how things are, since my attempt to do so will vainly try to pin things down as being one way rather than another.'[7]

I claim the Cyrenaics to be committed to the third of Lee's options, that is, indeterminacy. I make the additional claim that the Cyrenaics may have embraced both the kind of indeterminacy Lee refers to and another version of it, more radical, which account for the denial of the proper existence of objects. Contemporary speculation helps us to understand more appropriately what metaphysical indeterminacy amounts to in philosophical terms, as well as teaching us that even the most disturbing idea that there are no proper objects in the world could be accommodated within a credible theory of the material world.

For our own purposes here, it may be useful to refer once again to the dichotomy between mild and strong indeterminacy that has been introduced in Chapter 1.[8] We have seen that in current accounts of metaphysical indeterminacy, there are two kinds of it being discussed. One kind ('mild indeterminacy') maintains that material objects are indeterminate in their secondary qualities (hotness, redness, etc.); a second kind of indeterminacy ('radical indeterminacy') maintains that the world itself is indeterminate and deprived of material objects. If metaphysical indeterminacy is mild, we will be confronted with a vast array of material objects that are in themselves neither hot nor cold, neither sweet nor bitter and so on. If metaphysical indeterminacy is radical, we will be confronted with a vast array of undifferentiated matter, truly devoid of material objects.

We have seen in Chapter 1 that indeterminacy is at the core of Protagoras' Secret Doctrine and we are going to see in the Conclusion that indeterminacy is a fundamental element in ancient conceptions of ontological eliminativism. At the same time, in Chapter 4 I have offered a metaphysical reading of the Aristocles passage, one that commits Pyrrho to the view that things are not only undifferentiated and unstable, but also indeterminate. The kind of indeterminacy I attribute to Pyrrho may in principle accommodate both mild and radical indeterminacy. When things are said to be no more F, than not-F or both or neither is just another way to say that things are indeterminate in their secondary properties (mild indeterminacy). But even radical indeterminacy may easily come in in the picture: for the sort of reading I recommend, for Pyrrho material objects are not defined and are so undifferentiated one from the other that they can be regarded as not properly existent.[9]

The option of radical indeterminacy has also been brought to scholarly attention, exactly in connection with the Cyrenaics, by another important book, that is, Voula Tsouna, *The Epistemology of the Cyrenaic school* (Cambridge 1998). In her book, Tsouna suggests three metaphysical options seem to be potentially present in the philosophy of the Cyrenaics: (1) idealism; (2) the commonsensical view on whose basis the world is made up by ordinary objects and states of affairs; (3) 'radical indeterminacy' (she refers to it as the view that '[the material world is] an undifferentiated substratum affecting us in various ways').[10] As far as the metaphysics of the Cyrenaics is concerned, Tsouna rules out the idealist option, and I fully follow her lead on this.[11] She defends the second option, whereas I will defend the third one.

What I am about to do in the next sections is to see whether, in addition to the arguments I have made in Chapters 1, 2 and 4 to commit both Protagoras and Pyrrho to metaphysical indeterminacy, a credible case could be made to argue that the Cyrenaics too were indeterminists in metaphysics. In addition, while I construct a case for attributing indeterminacy to the Cyrenaics, I try to answer, mainly in the footnotes, to the criticism Tim O'Keefe (and, to some extent, Richard Bett) levels against the metaphysical reading of the Cyrenaics I advance.

Sextus and Colotes

After the brief survey into ancient and current conceptions of metaphysical indeterminacy, let us now go back to the passage of Sextus I have quoted at the opening, that is, *M.* VII 191-2. Let us briefly recapitulate where we were. The sceptical exegete of the Cyrenaics maintains that in that passage we are plainly given, by Sextus' own words, the essential details of Cyrenaic epistemology: for the Cyrenaics we know truly and infallibly how things appear to us, but not how things are in themselves. The contrast here is between infallible affections and inapprehensible items in the world. I have suggested that there are two possible ways to understand the claim that things are inapprehensible: either things are inapprehensible because we are distorted in our apprehension of them for a variety of factors (sceptical interpretation) or, alternatively, things are inapprehensible because by their own nature they are not determined, that is, there is nothing determinate there to be known for us (metaphysical interpretation).

On my understanding, Sextus' passage does not rule out any of the two interpretations. It simply insists that for the Cyrenaics affections can be known, while material things causing them cannot.[12] There is, however, another passage by Sextus that may support the indeterminacy reading of the Cyrenaics I suggest. The passage goes thus:

> Cyrenaic philosophers hold that affections alone exist [*mona huparchein ta pathē*] and nothing else. Since it is not an affection but rather it is something capable of producing an affection [*hothen kai tēn phōnēn mē ousan pathos, alla pathous poiētikēn*], sound is not one of the things that exist [*mē gignesthai tōn huparktōn*]. (*M.* VI 53=*SSR* IV A 219)

In this passage, Sextus reinterprets the Cyrenaic position on affections in metaphysical terms: the Cyrenaics grant existence to affections alone, whilst they deny proper existence to those things that cause our affections. We have sound-affections, but sound does not properly exist.[13] This passage is not usually given great importance because to deny existence to sensory-objects seems to be a rather awkward view to defend. But Sextus takes it seriously and attaches it not only to the Cyrenaics, but also to Plato and Democritus.[14] In addition, few lines after the long extract of Sextus I have quoted at the beginning of this chapter Sextus reports the same suspicion, from the Cyrenaics' part, about the actual existence of material objects. By reproducing the same dichotomy between affections and things that we have seen displayed in the opening lines of *M.* VII 191–2, Sextus remarks:

> We must therefore say either that the affections are the *phainomena* or that the things productive of the affections are the *phainomena*. If we say that the affections are the *phainomena*, we will have to maintain that all *phainomena* are true and apprehensible. If, on the contrary, we say that the things productive of the affections are the *phainomena*, all *phainomena* will be false and not apprehensible. The affection occurring in us tells us nothing more than itself. If one has to speak but the truth, the affection alone is therefore actually a *phainomenon* for us. What is external and productive of the affection [*to d'ektos kai tou pathous poiētikon*] perhaps is a being [*tacha men estin on*], but it is not a *phainomenon* for us. (*M.* VII 194=*SSR* IV A 213)

What causes our affections 'perhaps is a being'. This means that things in the world perhaps are not, properly speaking, existing items; that is, material things, as individual items, may well be not existent after all. After our survey into the notion of indeterminacy, to deny proper existence to material objects is understood as a quite serious philosophical view: we may think that in the two quoted passages Sextus is ascribing to the Cyrenaics a form of radical indeterminacy, on whose basis there are no proper objects (to be perceived) in the world.[15]

Is Sextus alone in attributing the Cyrenaics such a radical view? Not quite so, I claim. The oldest source on the Cyrenaics, a lengthy passage from the work of the Epicurean philosopher Colotes as preserved by Plutarch, suggests that the Cyrenaics may have embraced radical indeterminacy. I quote most of the passage:

> He [Colotes] aims, I suspect, to refute the Cyrenaics first, and then the Academy of Arcesilaus. The latter school was of those who suspended judgement on everything; whereas the former, placing all affections and sense-impressions within themselves, thought that the evidence derived from them was not enough, as far as assertions on external objects are concerned. Distancing themselves from external objects, they shut themselves up within their affections as in a siege. In doing so, they adopted the locution 'it appears' but refused to say in addition that 'it is' with regard

to external objects. This is the reason why – Colotes says – the Cyrenaics cannot live or cope with things. In addition, he says (making fun of them), that 'these men do not say that it/there is (*anthrôpon einai*) a man or a horse or a wall, but that they themselves are being walled or horsed or manned' [*toichousthai kai hippousthai kai anthrōpousthai*]. (*Adv. Col.* 1120c–d=*SSR* IV A 211)[16]

According to Plutarch, in his book entitled 'On the point that conformity to the views of other philosophers actually makes it impossible to live' Colotes singles out the Cyrenaics as a group of philosophers who make life impossible to live because of the doctrines they endorse. By granting epistemological infallibility to affections alone, the Cyrenaics shut themselves into a siege, distancing themselves from the external world. As Kechagia has observed, the Greek in the expression 'these men do not say that it/there is a man' (*anthrôpon einai*) is ambiguous and can be rendered with two different translations, depending on how one construes the verb '*einai*': either 'there is a man' in the existential sense of 'a man exists' or, alternatively, 'it is a man', meaning 'the thing here is a man'.

The ambiguity in the text provides us with two philosophical alternatives. Given the infallibility they grant to affections alone, the Cyrenaics refuse to say either that what causes our affections actually exists or, alternatively, that what produces in us an affection of sweet is, for instance, really honey. On the former alternative, Colotes would be denying existence to material objects; that is, he would be restating the same view that, at least on my interpretation, Sextus expresses in the two passages just quoted (hence committing the Cyrenaics to radical indeterminacy). On the second alternative, Colotes would be suggesting that the Cyrenaics cannot identify an external object as the kind of thing it is.[17]

Both Tsouna and Kechagia remark that both alternatives are well present in the text: Tsouna opts for the latter while Kechagia highlights the close philosophical linkage between the two options.[18] It is true that to refuse to identify an external object as the kind of thing it is different from saying that material things as such do not exist, but the former option may be well understood as leading, more or less naturally, to the latter. If in my affection of sweetness, I refuse to say that what produces in me that affection is really honey or a bar of chocolate; if in my affection of whiteness, I refuse to say whether it is either a table or a stone that produces that affection of white in me; what view of the material world could I end up to have? The most natural answer I can think of is that of a view of the world where objects play no part at all – since I cannot identify them for what they are. According to this view, we are confronted with an undifferentiated lump of matter, fully devoid of discrete items. And this is metaphysical indeterminacy, of the radical kind.

Colotes' reference to Cyrenaic neologisms, such as 'to be horsed', 'manned', leads Plutarch to complain that Colotes had not been historically accurate in reporting the doctrines of the Cyrenaics, since they are uniformly reported to have used neologisms referring to sensible qualities. While he recognizes that Colotes had actually put the fingers on the philosophical fulcrum of Cyrenaic philosophy, Plutarch insists he is able to expound such philosophy in more historically trustworthy terms.[19] But, I suggest, Colotes' real point has little to do with historical accuracy, much more with philosophical acumen. By using a slightly mocking tone, Colotes has correctly identified the main metaphysical feature of Cyrenaic philosophy, that is, the total absence of any reference to objects in their philosophy and in their philosophical language. If they want to make life possible, Colotes tells us, the Cyrenaics should restore in their philosophy the very notion of objects, which they appear to have wholly dispended with. Instead of using expressions referring to secondary qualities alone, and while retaining their original neologisms, the Cyrenaics should bring in expressions actually referring to objects such as horse and man. Otherwise, their philosophy would be completely untenable and make life actually impossible to live. This is, I claim, Colotes' quite sensitive appraisal of the Cyrenaics.

To avoid any reference to objects as such and to refer to the world of undifferentiated matter we are confronted with by indicating only secondary properties is exactly the best characterization of metaphysical indeterminacy according to what Aristotle says in *Metaphysics* 4, sections 5 and 6. When he deals with those who deny the principle of non-contradiction, Aristotle clearly shows that the principle of non-contradiction can be denied coherently only by those who assume that reality is ontologically indeterminate.[20] He suggests that those who deny the principle of non-contradiction and assume that reality is indeterminate get rid of, among other things, the notions of essence and substance, thus maintaining that everything has to be predicated *per accidens*. As Aristotle puts it:

And in general those who use this argument [i.e. those who deny the principle of non-contradiction] do away with substance and essence. For they must say that all attributes are accidents, and that there is no such thing as being essentially man or animal. For if there is to be any such thing as being essentially man this will not be being not-man or not being a man (yet these are negations of it); for there was some one thing which it meant, and this was the substance of something. And denoting the substance of a thing means that the essence of the thing is nothing else. But if its being essentially man is to be the same as either being essentially not-man or essentially not being a man, then its essence will be something else. Therefore our opponents must say that there cannot be such a definition of anything, but that all attributes are accidental; for this is the distinction between substance and accident – white is accidental to man, because though he is white, whiteness is not his essence. But if all statements are accidental, there will be nothing primary about which they are made, if the accidental always implies predication about a subject. (4.5.1007a21–b1)

According to Aristotle, thus, to refer to secondary qualities alone is the best mark of metaphysical indeterminacy. And to refer to secondary qualities alone is exactly what the Cyrenaics do when they use such neologisms as 'I am being whitened' (when they undergo a sensation of white, with reference to what is usually believed to be, for instance, a white chair). Again, despite his mocking tone, this is exactly the main point of Colotes' argument: the Cyrenaics should restore real objects in their metaphysics and, for that matter, in their neologisms if they wanted to make life possible to live.[21]

The Anonymous and Philodemus

I now turn briefly to two other passages that may lend support to my indeterminacy reading of the Cyrenaics. The first passage is a brief extract from the Anonymous' Commentary on Plato's *Theaetetus*. In that dialogue, while he explains the real meaning of Protagoras' maxim that man is the measure of all things, Socrates makes the example of the blowing wind (*Tht.* 152b1–3), which is felt as cold by someone and as hot by someone else. According to Protagoras' relativism, both perceivers are correct and legitimate in their different affections.[22] Socrates now asks Theaetetus the following metaphysical question: 'the wind itself, by itself, is cold or not cold? (152b5–6)'. In commenting on the question, the Anonymous remarks:

> Something is the agent, something else is the patient. But, if people undergo affections that are opposed to the thing in itself, they will agree that the intrinsic feature of the agent is not defined (*mê einai hôrismenên tên tou poiêsantos idiotêta*);[23] if it were so, the same thing at the same time will not produce different affections. Because of this, the Cyrenaics say that only affections are apprehensible, while external things are not. That I am being burnt, they say I apprehend; that the fire is such as to burn is obscure (*adelon*): if it were such, all things will be burnt by it. (col. LXV, 19–35=SSR IV A 214)

By suggesting a linkage, both terminological and conceptual, with the active and passive elements that are so central in the theory of perception endorsed by the subtler thinkers at *Theaetetus* 156a–157c, the Anonymous commentator remarks that, by being affected by the same object in different ways, it has to follow that 'the intrinsic feature of the agent is not defined'.[24] Material objects, therefore, are not ontologically determinate, since they (such as the wind of Socrates' example) may appear F to someone and not-F to someone else. Socrates' wind in itself is neither cold nor not-cold. It is simply neutral, that is, it does not possess any ontological feature of its own. On the basis of this explanation, the Cyrenaic view that affections alone are apprehensible relies on external objects being inapprehensible because ontologically indeterminate. The fire in itself is not caustic, because, if it were so, everybody would be burnt by it. It has to be noted here that the kind of indeterminacy that is ascribed to the Cyrenaics is mild, that is, objects are understood to be indeterminate as far as their secondary qualities are concerned.[25]

There is another source that has been brought to light by Tsouna as containing reference to the Cyrenaics. The passage in question does not name the Cyrenaics directly. However, Tsouna believes (quite correctly, I think) that the passage refers to the Cyrenaics.[26] The passage in question is by Philodemus of Gadara, an Epicurean philosopher, whose work *On Choices and Avoidances* (the title is conjectural) is preserved in a papyrus found in Herculaneum (PHerc. 1251, 23 columns). The papyrus is badly damaged so reconstruction by editors is often difficult. Philodemus probably wrote his treatise on choices in the first half of the first century BC, when the Cyrenaic school had already been dead for at least a century. A sensitive philosopher like Philodemus is capable to highlight the various developments the Cyrenaic school carried out in the elaboration of its philosophy over the space of more than two centuries. This is particularly probable in so far as the Cyrenaics, especially the later sects of the school, extensively rivalled the Epicureans with their theories on pleasure and the end. These Cyrenaic doctrines are likely to have been well known by those Epicureans, like Philodemus, who aimed to argue against them.

The main point Philodemus seems to be addressing in his text is a root-and-branch rejection of those philosophical doctrines that do not relate choices about actions to rational calculation and knowledge. In his attack against what he believes are irrational views that ground decisions for acting on factors that have nothing to do with reason and knowledge, Philodemus singles out a family of doctrines that are undoubtedly Cyrenaic in their core. The passage goes thus:

> (Col. II) They claim that as for truth no judgement is superior to any other. They believe in fact that the great *pathos* of the soul occurs as a result of pain and that thus we make our choices and avoidances by observing both bodily and mental pain (…)
>
> (Col. III) Some people denied that it is possible to know anything. They also added that if nothing on whose basis one should make an immediate choice is present, one should not choose immediately. Some other people made affections [*pathē*] of the soul as the moral ends and as not in need of any additional judgement based on further criteria. In doing so they granted to everybody an authority, which was not accountable, to get pleasure in whatever they cared to name and to do whatever contributed to it. Others held the view that what our school calls grief or joy are totally empty notions because of the manifest indeterminacy (*aoristia*) [of things]. (=SSR IV H 30)

The view that the affections of the soul are the ends of life (col. III) is the kernel of Cyrenaic ethics.[27] At the same time, Philodemus' words that affections are 'not in need of any additional judgement based on further criteria' is an explicit reference to the Cyrenaic idea that only affections are knowable and, from an epistemological standpoint, perfectly legitimate. In linking Cyrenaic ethics and epistemology in the way he does in the passage, Philodemus is concerned about the conceptual linkage he sees as operating between the ethics of the

Cyrenaics and their epistemology. Since they maintain that affections are the only source of knowledge, it will be correct for the Cyrenaics to postulate that people decide what course of action they will take in light of the affections they have. Given his rationalistic approach to ethics and knowledge, that one decides what action to perform on the basis of one's affections is a problematic view to adopt for Philodemus. While discussing these views, he also refers to a third group of people who appear to have criticized the Epicureans on the ground that what the Epicureans call grief or joy are 'totally empty notions because of the manifest indeterminacy [of things]' (end of col. III).[28] These people are highly likely to be exponents of later Cyrenaic sects, such as the Hegesians or the Theodorians, as Tsouna & Indelli and Dorandi have persuasively shown.[29]

Philodemus' attribution to the Cyrenaics of the view that things are indeterminate is quite remarkable. Philodemus attributes such indeterminacy to the Cyrenaics by making an example that has to do with ethical concepts, such as joy or grief, on which the Epicureans centred their ethical speculation. Although the attribution of indeterminacy to the Cyrenaics is made by suggesting an ethical example central to Epicurean thinking, Philodemus' attribution need not to be restricted to ethical cases at all. The attribution of the view that things are manifestly indeterminate comes at the end of Philodemus' reasoning against the Cyrenaics. This attribution appears to be the almost natural outcome of the whole argument Philodemus has been constructing in columns II and III, which is purported to criticize the philosophical views of the Cyrenaics.

I take such an argument to be the following. The Cyrenaics ground knowledge on affections; such affections cannot be further elaborated by reason and so are purely subjective. In being so, these affections grant to each of us the authority to take pleasure in whatever we believe (quite incorrectly, according to Philodemus) to be pleasurable. We thus decide for a particular course of action on the basis of our subjective affections. This is possible – that is the conclusive point when indeterminacy comes in – because things in the world are manifestly indeterminate: they are not in themselves pleasurable or painful, white or black and so on. On the basis of the conceptual reconstruction of Cyrenaic philosophy that Philodemus provides us with (at least on the ground of the interpretation I am offering), affections are for the Cyrenaics the basis of knowledge and the guide for action because things in the world are ultimately indeterminate.

Cyrenaic neologisms and indeterminacy

I have now constructed a case for showing that, in contrast with the sceptical reading, an alternative interpretation of the philosophy of the Cyrenaics is available. On the basis of the indeterminacy interpretation that I recommend, for the Cyrenaics only our affections are knowable not because we are somehow epistemologically incapable to arrive at the very nature of things, but, rather, because things in themselves are indeterminate. The responsibility here is on things, not on the knower. By drawing parallelisms with both ancient and contemporary conceptions of indeterminacy, I have suggested to interpret metaphysical indeterminacy mainly as tantamount to denying existence to material objects. I have shown that there is nothing in the sources that rules out the idea that the Cyrenaics could have actually been committed to indeterminacy. Even the passage from Sextus (*M*. VII 191–2) that is classically taken to expound the core of Cyrenaic subjectivism does not prevent us from assuming that the subjectivism endorsed by the Cyrenaics cannot in principle be rooted into a metaphysics of indeterminacy. On the contrary, other texts of Sextus and other important sources on the Cyrenaics do appear to commit them to indeterminacy.

A commitment to indeterminacy helps explaining those famous Cyrenaic neologisms we have often encountered in the course of the present chapter. When the Cyrenaic says: 'I am being whitened' or 'I am being sweetened', the sceptical exegete tends to take these sentences as an original way for expressing the epistemological subjectivism so inherent to Cyrenaic philosophy. With their neologisms, the sceptical argument goes, the Cyrenaics express the ultimate epistemological fact that we could know properly our internal states only, that is, how things affect us. But I find this argument not convincing. What strikes any reader (both modern and ancient) who hear Cyrenaic neologisms is the fact that, while proffering them, the Cyrenaics get rid of any reference to objects in the world. When I see a table as white or when I taste the honey as sweet, I usually say: 'I see that white table' or 'I taste this honey as sweet'. In both sentences there are two elements: the 'I', which refers to the person undergoing the affection (in this case, me), and the object that causes the relevant affection in me (table, honey). In the Cyrenaic neologism, like in our standard sentences reporting how we perceive things, the 'I' is there: so, on this respect, no Cyrenaic originality. The striking novelty of the Cyrenaic neologism lies in the expression 'to be whitened or sweetened', which fully replaces the talk of objects typical of our everyday language with a language that has no reference at all to objects. Perhaps this is the sort of language that also Pyrrho and the Heracliteans shoud have aimed for.[30]

My point here is not that I want to deny the salient characteristic of Cyrenaic epistemology (that is, its subjectivism), but, rather, to root it into a peculiar kind of metaphysics (that is, indeterminacy). Since things are radically indeterminate and are not, strictly speaking, existing items, the Cyrenaics may well maintain to be confronted with a world of undifferentiated matter affecting them in purely subjective ways. Differently from current treatments of metaphysical indeterminacy, the focus on the role of the subject could be the main feature of the metaphysics of indeterminacy as this was developed by the Cyrenaics.

On the contrary, to insist on the sceptical reading would mean to single out the epistemological view, deprived of any metaphysical connotation, as the main and only feature of Cyrenaic subjectivism. But this would mean more problems than originality for the Cyrenaics: how could the Cyrenaic proffering the expression 'I am being whitened' escape the danger of solipsism? How could that Cyrenaic know that there are other people in the world apart from him? In a Wittgensteinian fashion, how could that Cyrenaic know the very nature and content of his own affections if he could be the sole existent being in the world? Could he build up a credible way to detect and understand his own affections if he has no way to escape his solipsism? I try to answer these questions in the following chapter.[31]

To say that the Cyrenaics accompany their epistemology with a traditional outlook of the material world is, I believe, a too unwarranted answer to these questions, also given the fact that an alternative reading is there, a reading that I claim is more promising to make sense of Cyrenaic philosophy as a whole. If we want to understand the Cyrenaics as sceptics, we should be prepared to look at them as sceptics in the sense that Richard Bett has attached to Pyrrho (although Bett does not think the Cyrenaics to be sceptics of this kind).[32] They would have anticipated, in different way and perhaps with different aims, Pyrrho's metaphysical thesis as this is shown in Chapter 4 (as well as siding with the metaphysical views on which Protagoras' Secret Doctrine is centred). And this new perspective would help us not only rethink the philosophical importance of the Cyrenaics in Greek philosophy, but also reconsidering the history and development of ancient scepticism in a new light.

6

The Cyrenaics on solipsism and privacy

As we have seen in the Introduction, when talking about eliminativism or nihilism in the context of this book, no distinction has been made between objects and persons. This is the case not because a distinction is not theoretically possible but mainly because to understand the ontological status of persons in both Greek and Buddhist philosophies is a topic that requires a book in itself (as I have said, I hope it will be the sequel to this one). Yet, an exception to the rule of not distinguishing between material objects and people that I have routinely followed in this book has to be made for the Cyrenaics.

On the understanding I have provided in the previous chapter, against rival, more conservative readings, I have claimed that in parallel with their theory of affections, the Cyrenaics endorsed a theory of metaphysical indeterminacy about material objects. For the Cyrenaics, the world out there, of material objects and determinate items, is somehow lost in a distant fog; on the contrary, the internal world of our own perceptions, is by contrast, vividly and only truly present to us. It is the theoretical as well as practical predominance of the internal versus the external that makes the Cyrenaics, again on some interpretations, as the discoverers of the notion of subjectivity in the ancient world.[1]

It is thus well worth asking what view of subjectivity the Cyrenaics may have endorsed, in the context of their eliminativism about material objects. If material objects are, at best, elusive items such that I cannot really understand what causes my feeling of hotness in me right now is fire or some other objects;[2] if the only thing I am truly and infallibly aware of is that I am now feeling hot (that is, that I am being warmed, in Cyrenaic jargon);[3] if each of us has their own feelings, which are not accessible to others;[4] if all this is the case, the conclusion will be that the only word that is truly real is mine;

as Wittgenstein would put it: 'Mine is the first and only world' (Notebook, 2 September 1916). Solipsism would be, after all, a true view for the Cyrenaics.

Solipsism is a doctrine that has had very few adherents. Yet, it does have a philosophical appeal that invites us to take it seriously. As Sami Pihlström has recently argued, there are many kinds of solipsism in philosophy: from metaphysical to epistemological, from logical to semantic (with the further dichotomy 'strong/mild' to introduce other sub-classes to be included in the general taxonomy).[5] At the same time, as far as the actual liveability of solipsism is concerned, we are all debtors to the arguments Rae Langton has offered to show that, when treating other persons as objects (as e.g., in sexual objectification and pornography), we do live solipsistic lives, however difficult it may be to motivate solipsism theoretically.[6] Even if the *theory* of solipsism is difficult to be coherently formulated, the *practice* of solipsism is more widespread than we are inclined to think at a first sight.

To my knowledge, there has been so far no attempt in the scholarship to address the problem of solipsism in ancient philosophy. This is unexpected, given the evident vitality of the scholarship in this area. It is also surprising, since as I have briefly said, the Cyrenaics seem, at least *prima facie*, to advance philosophical views where solipsism is either implied or easily accommodated into.[7] The aim of this chapter is to assess the evidence on Cyrenaic solipsism and show how and why some views endorsed by the Cyrenaics appear to be committing them to solipsism. After evaluating the fascinating case for Cyrenaic solipsism, I shall deal with an (often) underestimated argument on language attributed to the Cyrenaics, whose logic – if I reconstruct it well – implies that after all the Cyrenaics cannot have endorsed a radical solipsism. Yet, by drawing an illuminating parallel with Wittgenstein's argument on private language and inner sensations, a case is to be made for the Cyrenaics to have subscribed to a sort of 'residual solipsism', which in turn helps us to understand the notion of Cyrenaic privacy at a fuller extent.

Solipsism

One of the main things to be noted when talking of solipsism is that it is a label that covers many different views, with many of us adopting a rather monolithically shaped version of it, such as 'I alone exist'.[8] For this reason, I shall be inevitably selective and provide some definitions on solipsism that I think are particularly apt for the Cyrenaics. Here is a quotation from Todd (1968, p. vii):

> The solipsist does not deny that there are reasons for believing in the existence of the external world and the existence of other persons (…). He is saying that one can admit all this and still not commit oneself ontologically to anything beyond the occurrence of one's own sensations and certain principle governing them. Thus, while the modern solipsist would never deny the existence of the world, his hypothesis is that we can assert its existence just by talking ultimately about our own sensations and making very complex assertions about them. His views is that we never have beliefs which commit us to anything more than this (…). Instead of denying the existence of an irreducible physical world he tells us that we never believed in it anyway.

Here there is another quotation, from Rollins (Rollins 1967, p. 488):

> [For the solipsist] Every claim concerning the existence or nonexistence of anything is grounded in experience and could not possibly extend beyond it. An existential claim which seemed to reach beyond experience could have no basis or reference; it would apparently be unintelligible and not strictly a claim at all. But experience is essentially immediate; in itself it is never mistaken (…) and it is had by one person truly and is private to him. Hence, existential claims can never truly, and perhaps never with full intelligibility, claim more than the existence of the experiencing self and its states, and indeed perhaps never claim more than this as of the moment of experience.[9]

By relying on these two characterization of solipsism, which are centred on the epistemological indispensability of one's own affections to make any existential claim about 'the world', I shall assess the plausibility of Cyrenaic solipsism.

Cyrenaic solipsism I: Colotes

On the interpretation I shall be sketching in the following sections, a case seems to be made for Cyrenaic solipsism. There are two major sources that point to Cyrenaic solipsism. The first main source is a passage from Plutarch's *Against*

Colotes, which I have partially quoted in the previous chapter. In his attempt to show that all those philosophers who do not adhere to Epicurus' doctrines make life impossible to live, Colotes targets, among others, the Cyrenaics too. In reporting Colotes' views, Plutarch writes:

> He (*sc.* Colotes) aims, I suspect, to refute the Cyrenaics first, and then the Academy of Arcesilaus. The latter school was of those who suspended judgement on everything; whereas the former, placing all affections and sense-impressions within themselves, thought that the evidence derived from them was not enough, as far as assertions on external objects are concerned. Distancing themselves from external objects, they shut themselves up within their affections as in a siege. In doing so, they adopted the locution 'it appears' but refused to say in addition that 'it is' with regard to external objects. This is the reason why – Colotes says – the Cyrenaics cannot live or cope with things. In addition, he says (making fun of them), that 'these men do not say that a man or a horse or a wall is, but that they themselves are being walled or horsed or manned (*toichousthai kai hippousthai kai anthrôpousthai*)' (1120c-d=*SSR* IV A 211).[10]

Plutarch comments on Colotes' understanding of the Cyrenaics:

> In the first place, Colotes uses these expressions maliciously, just as a professional denouncer would do. These consequences among others will follow without any doubt from the teachings of the Cyrenaics. He should however have presented their doctrine in the actual form in which those philosophers taught it. They say we are being sweetened and bittered and chilled and warmed and illuminated and darkened (*glukainesthai gar legousi kai pikrainesthai kai psuchesthai kai thermainesthai kai phôtizesthai kai skotizesthai*). Each of these affections has within itself its own evidence, which is intrinsic to it and unchallenged (*tôn pathôn toutôn hekastou tên enargeian oikeian en hautôi kai aperispaston echontos*). But whether the honey is sweet or the young olive-shoot bitter or the hail chilly or the unmixed wine warm or the sun luminous or the night air dark is contested by many witnesses (wild and domesticated animals and humans too). Some in fact dislike honey, others like olive-shoots or are burned off by hail or are chilled by the wine or go blind in the sunlight and see well at night. When opinion stays close to the affection it therefore preserves its infallibility (*hothen emmenousa tois pathesin ê doxa diatêrei to anamart êton*). On the contrary, when it oversteps them and mixes up with judgements and statements about external objects,

it often disturbs itself and makes a fight against other people, who receive from the same objects contrary affections and different sense-impressions. (1120e-f= *SSR* IV A 211)

Colotes accuses the Cyrenaics of making life impossible because of their sceptical epistemology. Plutarch laments that Colotes uses some expressions (that is, 'to be horsed', 'manned' or 'walled') as referred to the Cyrenaics in a malicious way, because (he warns) Colotes should have presented the Cyrenaic doctrine in the actual way they did. Yet, Plutarch highlights that the consequences Colotes emphasizes do follow from the teachings of the Cyrenaics. In fact, as other sources tell us, the Cyrenaics used expressions such as 'to be sweetened', 'chilled', 'warmed' and so on to express the absolute, unquestionable legitimacy of one's own *pathê*. When I see something as white, or when I taste something as sweet, or when I feel something as warm, instead of reverting to the traditional linguistic usage and saying, 'This honey is sweet'; 'The sun is warm'; 'Your face is white', by following the Cyrenaic neologism I should say: 'I am being whitened', 'I am being warmed', 'I am being sweetened'.[11]

As said in the previous chapter, the main philosophical point in these neologisms is that no reference is ever made to those external objects that are supposed to be causing the *pathos* of 'whiteness', 'sweetness' and 'warmth' in us. This is the case, Colotes warns, because the Cyrenaics think that the sort of evidence we can derive from the way things appear to us is not enough, as far as legitimate assertions on external objects are concerned. In his comments Plutarch gives further explanation about Colotes' remark by insisting that the second-order judgements we construe on the basis of how things appear to us preserve their infallibility when they stay close to the immediacy of affection. On the contrary, when we move from the immediacy of how things appear to us to judgements and statements about (the material identity of) external objects, we are immediately trapped in a battle of conflicting appearances that gives us no clue whatsoever on how things really are. Both Colotes and Plutarch are thus in agreement and are both right in identifying the kernel of Cyrenaic epistemology as the view that only (our) *pathê* are known to us and are epistemologically infallible, while the things that are supposed to cause those *pathê* in us are not.

If this is the case, the Cyrenaic individual is, indeed, the sort of solipsist that Todd and Rollins describe in the two quotations above. He claims that his experience (his affections, how he is affected) is never mistaken and is, indeed, private to him. The world out there perhaps exists, but it is something the Cyrenaic individual cannot have a real grip on. What can be claimed in the Cyrenaic world is that, as Rollins writes, 'existential claims can never truly, and perhaps never with full intelligibility, claim more than the existence of the experiencing self and its states, and indeed perhaps never claim more than this as of the moment of experience'. On the basis of this interpretation, solipsism is thus the main reason for which Colotes thinks the Cyrenaics make life impossible, since it is solipsism that traps them into a sort of privacy, either epistemological or ontological, which prevents them from living a truly real life.

Cyrenaic solipsism II: Aristocles of Messene

While the Cyrenaics were fiercely criticized by the Epicurean Colotes, they also got a critical coverage by the peripatetic philosopher Aristocles of Messene. In an extant section of his *On Philosophy*, Aristocles rephrases Colotes' charge that life is impossible for the Cyrenaics from an Aristotelian standpoint. Again, it is the kind of solipsism inherent to Cyrenaic doctrines that, according to Aristocles, makes life impossible to live. He writes:

> Next would be those who say that affections alone are apprehensible (*mona ta pathê katalêpta*). This view was adopted by some of the philosophers from Cyrene. As if oppressed by a kind of torpor, they maintained that they knew nothing at all, unless someone standing beside them struck and pricked them. They said that, when burnt or cut, they knew that they were affected by something (*kaiomenoi gar elegon ê temnomenoi gnôrizein hoti paschoien*). But whether the thing which is burning them is fire, or that which cut them is iron, they could not tell (*poteron de to kaion eiê pur ê to temnon sidêros, ouk echein eipein*). (Eusebius, *PE* 14. 19. 1=*SSR* IV A 218=Chiesara F5)

What is striking here is that, after reaffirming the kernel of Cyrenaic epistemology, Aristocles uses an image to describe the approach the Cyrenaic individual has to the external world that is so reminiscent of the sort of detachment Colotes conveys with the image of the Siege. For Aristocles, the Cyrenaics claim to know nothing at all, not even that there are other people and an external world, unless someone struck or pricked them. What they do know is how they are being affected, that is, burnt or cut. But they cannot go beyond the limit of their own affections and tell that what is burning them is fire or that what is cutting them is iron. Again, the radical option about the external world being indeterminate: the Cyrenaic individual is unaware of external objects as they are, since what he can know is how he is affected, not what affects him. The Cyrenaic individual lives in the world of his own affections and is thus incapable to escape its ontological limits because he does not have a clue about the actual existence of external objects. Not only is he in the position to elaborate on solipsism, but also *lives* his own solipsism by being isolated from the outside world in an uninterrupted torpor.[12]

Aristocles brings out what he thinks are the absurdities arising from these Cyrenaic views:

> Three things must necessarily exist at the same time: the affection itself (*to te pathos auto*), what causes it (*to poioun*), and what undergoes it (*to paschon*). The person who apprehends an affection must necessarily perceive also what undergoes it. It cannot be the case that, if someone is for example warm, one will know that one is being warmed without knowing whether it is himself or a neighbour, now or last year, in Athens or Egypt, someone alive or dead, a man or a stone. One will therefore know too what one is affected by, for people know one another and the roads, cities, the food they eat. Likewise, craftsmen know their tools, doctors and sailors infer by means of signs what will happen, and dogs discover the tracks of wild animals. (Eusebius *PE* 14. 19.3-4=no corresponding testimony in *SSR*=Chiesara F5)

Aristocles thus believes that if he adheres to his doctrines, the Cyrenaic individual will be unable to get a proper grasp of both poles of the perceptual process: either who is being affected or what is being affected by.[13] Closed up in his solipsism, the Cyrenaic individual does not have a clue about what is affected by (he is being warmed but he does not know whether it is a wind or a hairdryer that makes him feel warm). Conversely, if we follow closely Aristocles' argument, the Cyrenaic individual does not even know the actual, ontological identity of himself as the perceptual agent. This is the case – Aristocles argues – because not only does the external world become an elusive item in the perceptual process but also because by insisting on the absolute subjectivism of perceptual states, the Cyrenaics end up dissipating the ontological relevance of the subject as an aggregate of temporary, evanescing affections. The Cyrenaic individual is one of the items of the material world, together with other (external) objects – so Aristocles may have argued. In other words, if solipsism is the view that Aristocles sees as arising from Cyrenaicism, he seems to be construing a case to make that solipsism as refuted by internal grounds.[14]

Internal touch

I am not going to discuss the legitimacy of Aristocles' criticism. More in general, I am not going to address how the Cyrenaics may have responded to the charges levelled against them, because my main aim in this chapter is to understand on what grounds we may think that the Cyrenaics endorsed solipsism, not what counterarguments they would have used to defend their solipsistic views from criticism. What I want to highlight is that both Colotes (with Plutarch) and Aristocles motivate their claims that the Cyrenaics made life impossible by insisting on the fact that their own doctrines confine the Cyrenaic individual into a solipsistic corner, while making the Cyrenaic individual the measure of his own world.

The point about the Cyrenaic individual being the criterion of truth and existence is brought forward by Cicero in two related passages from the *Academica*, which have often been duly underestimated:

> What about touch, of that touch philosophers call interior (*interiorem*), of either pleasure or pain, in which the Cyrenaics believe that only there is the criterion of truth (*iudicium*), because it is perceived by means of the senses? (*Ac. Pr.* II 7, 20=SSR IV A 209)

> What about the Cyrenaics, by no means contemptible philosophers? They deny that anything can be perceived from the outside (*qui negant esse quicquam quod percipi posit extrinsecus*), while they do say to perceive only those things they experience by means of an internal touch (*ea sola percipere quae tactu intumo sentiant*), like pain and pleasure; they cannot know whose sound or colour something is, but to sense only to be affected in a certain way. (*Ac. Pr.* II 24, 76=SSR IV A 209)

Cicero is the only source to mention the interior touch in relation to the Cyrenaics. However elusive the concept of '*tactus intumus* or *interior*' may be, it is clear from Cicero's passages that the Cyrenaic individual is the ultimate measure of his own world in so long as he knows and acts on the sole basis of his affections. This is the case for both 'ethical' affections (of pleasure and pain) and for the larger class of 'epistemological' affections (of sounds, colours and so on). Sedley notes: 'in Hellenistic philosophy, "internal touch" emerges as a technical term for the sense that makes us *directly aware of changes going inside us*' (my emphasis).[15] This being the case, each of us has his own internal touch that is responsible for the actual ways we are privately affected. Given the strict subjectivism the Cyrenaics grant to one's perceptions and sensations, it looks as if we all live in different private worlds shaped by our internal touches, with no access to the inner world of others.

From different historical and philosophical perspectives, all the sources analysed thus far contribute to creating the image of the Cyrenaics as philosophers very much inclined to take solipsism as a view somehow inherent to their philosophy. On the ground of the case I have been constructing so far, the Cyrenaics can thus be taken as the true and real solipsists of the ancient (Western) world.[16]

The commonality of language: Sextus on the Cyrenaics

This image is challenged by a long passage of Sextus Empiricus, which I shall give in full considering its importance:

> [For the Cyrenaics] No criterion is common to human beings, common names are assigned to objects (*onomata de koina tithesthai tois chrêmasin*). (196) All in common in fact call something white or sweet (*leukon men gar ti kai gluku kalousi koinôs pantes*), but they do not have something common that is white or sweet (*koinon de ti leukon ê gluku ouk echousin*). Each human being is aware of his own private affection (*hekastos gar tou idiou pathous antilambanetai*). One cannot say, however, whether this affection occurs in oneself and in one's neighbour from a white object (*to de ei touto to pathos apo leukou enginetai autôi kai tôi pelas*), since one cannot grasp the affection of the neighbour, nor can his neighbour, since he cannot feel the affection of that other person. (197) And since no affection is common to us all, it is hasty to declare that what appears to me a certain way appears the same way to my neighbour as well. Perhaps I am constituted so as to be

whitened by the external object when it comes into contact with my senses, while another person has the senses constructed so as to have been disposed differently. In any case, the *phainomenon* is absolutely not common to us all (*ou pantôs oun koinon esti to phainomenon hêmin*). (198) That we really are not all affected in the same way because of different dispositions of our senses is clear from the cases of people who suffer from jaundice or ophthalmia and from those who are in a natural condition. Just as the first group of persons are affected yellowly, the second redly and third whitely from the same thing, so it is also probable that those who are in a natural condition are not affected in the same way by the same things because of the different construction of their senses, but rather that the person with grey eyes is affected in one way, the one with blue eyes in another, and the one with black eyes in another yet different way. It follows that the names we assign to things are common (*hôste koina men hêmas onomata tithenai tois pragmasin*), but that we have private affections (*pathê de ge echein idia*). (*M.* 7. 195-98=*SSR* IV A 213)

This passage is important for two main reasons: for what it says and for what it does not say. I shall start from what it says. Sextus confirms the main tenets of Cyrenaic philosophy when he reports the usual Cyrenaic view that each of us is solely and uniquely aware of his own affections, without being able either to have access to the affection of others or to say that the object causing the affection is really as we perceive it. Again, the Cyrenaic individual is aware (in a solipsistic way) of what he feels, with no actual access to the real world out there or to the inner world of others. Yet, the Cyrenaic individual – and this is the main novelty that the passage introduces – shares with others 'common names': 'common names are assigned to objects'; 'names we assign to things are common' (see the beginning and end of Sextus' passage).[17]

The fact that we have common names means that the Cyrenaic individual is not equipped with a private language to name his own affections.[18] The actual dichotomy the passage introduces is one between 'common names' and 'private affections', so that what is being highlighted is that, although we have private affections that are neither relatable to the actual way things are nor to the way other people perceive things, we are in the condition to call our private affections with common names. Remember that the Cyrenaics invented such neologisms as 'I am being whitened' or 'I am being sweetened'. These expressions are 'common names' for the Cyrenaics: we all learn to call something as 'white' or 'sweet' (or to be more accurate, we all learn how to use the expressions 'to be sweetened or whitened'), although we do refer to different (private) affections.[19]

There is therefore something that is common in the Cyrenaic world: at least a public language exists! The Cyrenaic individual can still be in the position to defend his own solipsistic views because the fact that a common language is spoken does not exclude that the Cyrenaic individual is the only and actual measure of his world. If we refer back to the idea of living a solipsistic life (in contrast with the difficulty to motivate it theoretically) which I briefly introduced at the beginning of this chapter, we can say that the Cyrenaic individual may well be in the position to live it, despite being forced to admit that a communal language is spoken.

Is this communal language simply spoken or is it *to be* spoken? That is, do we need a public language to be able to account for our own private affections? And with this question I turn to the second aspect of Sextus' passage, that is, what it does not say. Sextus constructs an argument purported to show that despite being centred on an absolute and un-transferrable privacy, Cyrenaic epistemology admits of a public, shared language, to refer and name individual affections. But how is it so? How is it possible that the Cyrenaic individual can name his own private affections by means of a public language? Sextus does not say anything about this, and we are left wondering. Even the probable commitment to conventionalism on the part of the Cyrenaics does not help us on the matter. We may all agree to call something conventionally (as e.g., 'chair') but this does not tell us how we manage to do so as far as sensations and perceptions are concerned. For anyone familiar with contemporary philosophy, the need to bring in relevant discussions from Wittgenstein becomes inevitable. He is the philosopher who has so far managed to develop the most influential argument about public languages and inner sensations. What I thus propose at this point is to move onto a more speculative terrain, to assess how Wittgenstein's treatment of the very same topics that we see as discussed in Sextus' passage may further illuminate the problem of solipsism, either in itself or in connection with the Cyrenaics.

Wittgenstein's Private Language argument: A Trojan horse for Cyrenaic solipsism?

Wittgenstein is perhaps the contemporary philosopher who flirted with solipsism more than any others, from the *Tractatus*, via the *Blue Book,* to the *Philosophical Investigations*.[20] More perspicuously, his notorious argument about the impossibility of a private language to name private, inner sensations is to be read not only as his most sophisticated attempt to argue against the sort of solipsistic temptations he had felt so acutely since writing the *Tractatus*, but also, and more relevantly here, as a stimulating comparison with the argument about private affections and common names that in the quoted passage Sextus develops in connection with the Cyrenaics.

The philosophical problems that Wittgenstein considers in the sections of the *Philosophical Investigations* devoted to discussing the (im)possibility of a private language are remarkably similar to a problem that the Cyrenaics may have well faced: how can one name his inner, private sensations? How can a person identify, re-identify, and name his sensations? Wittgenstein starts off by imagining a solipsistic case that, once again, can be the actual one the Cyrenaic individual may have well faced. Wittgenstein makes the example of a diarist who wants to keep a diary about the recurrence of a certain sensation:

> To this end I associate it [the sensation] with the sign 'S' and write this sign in a calendar for every day on which I have the sensation (…). I speak, or write the sign down, and at the same time I concentrate my attention on the sensation – and so, as it were, point to it inwardly. – but what is this ceremony for? For that is all it seems to be! A definition surely serves to establish the meaning of a sign. – Well, that is done precisely by the concentrating of my attention; for in this way I impress on myself the connexion between the sign and the sensation. – but 'I impress it on myself' can only mean: this process brings it about that I remember the connexion right in the future. But in the present case I have no criterion of correctness. One would like to say: whatever is going to seem right to me is right. And that only means that here we can't talk about 'right'. (*PI*, § 258)

The solipsistic diarist cannot name a sensation he has with a private 'sign' because this would put him in the condition of not being able to find out a correct criterion to re-identify that sensation. His private 'sign' for the sensation

'S' would not give it any plausible criterion of correctness. To understand, account for and name our sensations – Wittgenstein argues – we need to rely on objective, publicly shared criteria. Wittgenstein makes the example of a manometer that registers a rise of someone's blood pressure when one has a particular sensation (*PI*, § 270). Or he refers to the case of someone who does not know whether he correctly remembers the departure time for a train. If this person recalls to his mind the mental image of the timetable he once looked at, this will not be enough because 'the mental image of the time-table could not itself be tested for correctness' (*PI*, § 265). That person would need to look at the actual timetable, which is publicly checkable, to be sure of the correct departure time for his train.

While showing that it is impossible to create a private language for inner sensations because there would be no criteria of correctness available for the use of such a language, Wittgenstein also develops a view about the semantics of sensations that Ayer believes to be even more radical than Carnap's crude verificationism. As Ayer puts it: 'He [Wittgenstein] seems to take the view that someone who attempted to use language in this private way would not merely be unable to communicate his meaning to others but would have no meaning to communicate even to himself; he would not succeed in saying anything at all'.[21] This person would not only be unable to name his own sensations but also, and more essentially, he would be in the unpleasant position not to understand what kind of sensation he is dealing with. As Wittgenstein writes to make the point, 'you learned the concept *pain* when you learned language' (*PI*, § 384).[22] He insists that every concept we employ, including those related to sensations, is mediated through the communal language we use and the language-games we all play and share.[23]

There is a huge bibliography on Wittgenstein's private language argument, which is undoubtedly one of the most famous arguments in contemporary philosophy.[24] I do not have any pretence either to deal with the many philosophical issues the private language argument raises or to confront the extensive scholarship on it. Yet, for our own purposes here, Wittgenstein offers a powerful argument against solipsism when he argues that we all learn the names of our sensations and perceptions by means of a shared, common language and that it cannot really be otherwise. If we move back to the case of the Cyrenaics, it will have to be noted that Sextus' passage insists on the commonality of language in relation to the privacy of individual affections, thus arguing that for the Cyrenaics we have private affections but common names (which we all use to refer to private affections).

There is no way for us to understand how the Cyrenaics motivated this view, but it is strikingly like the one Wittgenstein develops in the *Philosophical Investigations* to argue against a private language. For both the Cyrenaics and Wittgenstein, we have common names for our sensations and perceptions.[25] Wittgenstein gives us compelling arguments to defend the view that it is impossible for us to understand and name our sensations privately (or in a solipsistic way). The Cyrenaics do not do that, but the insistence on the commonality of a shared language to name our sensations and perceptions cannot point if not in the same direction of Wittgenstein's argument. It is only by relying on common names that we can make sense of our internal, private world of affections: this is the view that, I claim, can be ascribed to the Cyrenaics on the basis of Sextus' passage.[26]

If this is the case, the commitment to solipsism on the part of the Cyrenaics will be seriously jeopardized. If all our private affections are mediated and informed by the language we all speak and the conceptual schemes inherent to it, this will entail that the privacy of one's affections relies on other people having other private affections, equally valuable and legitimate. Despite insisting on the privacy of one's affections, the Cyrenaics must have been prepared to admit that the plurality of private affections different people have does pose a quite serious philosophical challenge for those philosophers like them claiming that there is an insuperable gulf between my perceptions and those of others. After all, despite having private affections, we all learn their grammar and how to understand them by relying on a public tool, namely our shared language.

If read along quite plausible interpretative lines as the ones suggested above, Sextus' argument on the commonality of language therefore seems to reduce the Cyrenaic commitment to solipsism in a drastic way. Yet, the case for Cyrenaic solipsism that I have been constructing in the previous sections of this chapter still rests on a highly plausible reading of the extant evidence. How can we make sense of this clash? Again, a crucial distinction Wittgenstein introduces between the epistemological privacy and the privacy of the ownership will help to make the clash an apparent one, while also making a case for a sort of residual solipsism in Cyrenaic philosophy by spelling out more clearly what the Cyrenaics may have actually meant when they talked of 'private affections' (*pathê idia*).

Residual solipsism: The inalienable privacy of the ownership

When he deals with the privacy of sensations in the context of the private language argument, Wittgenstein makes a clear distinction between epistemological privacy and the privacy of the ownership:[27] as Hacker writes, for Wittgenstein 'something is epistemologically private for a person if only he can know it; it is private in the second sense [that is, privacy of the ownership] if, in principle only he can have it' (Hacker 1972, p. 231).[28] On the basis of this distinction, we understand that for Wittgenstein epistemological privacy is impossible while the privacy of the ownership is unalienable: I can well know that others are in pain while it does not make sense to say, 'I know I am in pain', since the conditions of knowledge/doubt do not hold for first-person statement about one's inner sensations. I cannot say: 'I have pain and I don't know it' and thus I cannot say: 'I have pain and I know it'. What I can say without any doubt is that I *have* a pain, namely, that the pain I feel is simply and only my own and cannot be someone else's.[29]

If we apply Wittgenstein's dichotomy about privacy (epistemological vs. of the ownership) to the Cyrenaics, at first, we may be thinking that both privacies are legitimate for them. But this would be wrong. As we already know by now, the kernel of Cyrenaic epistemology is that only (private) affections are known to us. When they say that I cannot be mistaken that I am being whitened, the Cyrenaics must admit – one can argue – that I know that I am having an affection of white. Yet, what is being known for the Cyrenaics is the actual affection we are having, not that we know that we are affected. To say that we know we are being whitened would be as pleonastic and redundant for the Cyrenaics as it would be senseless for Wittgenstein. The Cyrenaics may have been uninterested in the notion of epistemological privacy, at least in Wittgenstein's sense, but they surely endorsed the privacy of the ownership for affections. The Cyrenaics thought that I surely have and own my sensation of white or pain when I say: 'I am being whitened' or 'I feel pain'. When they insist on the privacy of one's affections, what I claim the Cyrenaics are highlighting is that each of us possesses his own sensation and that we cannot have (any access whatsoever to) the sensations of others: I cannot have/feel your pain. As Sextus remarks: '[for the Cyrenaics] one cannot grasp the affection of the neighbour, nor can his neighbour, since he cannot feel the affection of that other person' (*M.* 7.196).

One may retort that there is an epistemological aspect involved in the insistence the Cyrenaics place on the privacy of affections, since they make clear that the actual ownership of a sensation brings with it the inescapable epistemological certainty about the infallibility of that sensation. For the Cyrenaics, I cannot be mistaken that I am being whitened; that is, in modern parlance, I cannot be mistaken that I see that object as white. The inalienability of the ownership of affections does not exclude, however, that an epistemological aspect is involved in the process. Quite the contrary, I suggest. When we claim that a sensation is inalienable, we may well mean that each of us has his own sensation (either of 'red' or 'pain') and that we cannot *have* the sensation of others. Accordingly, we cannot *know* whether the actual sensation we have is identical or different from the one someone else has. We cannot know where my sensation of red or pain is identical or different from yours. Following Wittgenstein (and, on the interpretation sketched in this chapter, the Cyrenaics too), we can submit that you and I have learned how to name our sensations by means of a communal language, so that we have common names for private affections. Yet, you and I will never know whether the common names we use for our affections name identical or different sensations. As Wittgenstein writes: 'The essential thing about private experience is really not that each person possesses his own exemplar, but that nobody knows whether other people also have *this* or something else. The assumption would thus be possible – though unverifiable – that one section of mankind had one sensation of red and another section another' (*PI*, § 272).

There is therefore a residual solipsism about private affections that rests on the inalienability of their ownership and that no communal language or shared semantic criteria can ever get rid of. We may have common names for private affections (as the Cyrenaics maintain, according to Sextus); we may well map our internal world of perceptions and sensations by means of a public language (as Wittgenstein argues). Yet, each of us *has* his own private sensations and perceptions. There really seems to be no way to assess whether we have different or the same ones, although we have common names to refer to them. Although we use common names and public languages, I cannot have any access to your own sensations, and you cannot feel mine. This fact contributes much to the idea that there is a subjective privacy that is at the core of whom we are. It is this privacy that contributes, in an essential way, to the actual constitution of our inner self. If we pair such a privacy with the features of epistemological incorrigibility; if we discharge the material world of objects and other people as wholly elusive, we shall start to realize how innovative and original the Cyrenaics could have been. For the first time in Greek philosophy, they highlighted the importance of the subject as the locus of inner life, despite being ready to recognize that, at least on the interpretation I recommend, the subject lacked a deeper identity, ontologically stable over time.[30] They made that subject the fulcrum of their epistemological and ethical life, in contrast with a world of material objects whose indeterminate essence they thought could never be grasped. They believed that each of us has his own, inalienable inner world, to which others cannot have any access despite common names and public languages. In doing so, the Cyrenaics were the kind of solipsist philosophers who Wittgenstein describes in the *Blue Book* and for whom I cannot see, hear or feel, what others see, hear or feel.[31]

Although they may have not endorsed the sort of encompassing solipsism that I have tried to ascribe to them in the initial sections of this chapter, the residual solipsism that I identified in this last section is at the core of the originality that Cyrenaic philosophy has displayed over the centuries. Such residual solipsism is, I claim, what can motivate the main philosophical views around which the Cyrenaics built up their philosophy and their notion of inalienable privacy.

Conclusion: Eliminativism, indeterminacy and nihilism between East and West

Eliminativism in Greek and Buddhist philosophies

This book has aimed to provide a genealogy of, and a context for, ontological eliminativism in ancient philosophy by looking with some fresh eyes at some textual evidence about Protagoras and Gorgias, Pyrrho and the Cyrenaics, Vasubandhu and Nāgārjuna. More than descriptive, my approach has been revisionary in so long as I have tried to make good philosophical and historical sense of a neglected tradition in ancient thought by linking comparatively Eastern and Western traditions. I hope my effort has brought out, partially but also substantially, the richness and variety of a metaphysical position that is worth investigating in the context of ancient thought as well as for its possible relevance in contemporary debate in metaphysics.

As far as ancient Greek philosophy is concerned, ontological eliminativism appears to be a much less developed tradition than, for instance, the ontologies of Plato, Aristotle and the Stoics – at least this is what the scanty evidence *tells* us. It may however well be the case that we may be here dealing with deceptive appearances; historically, ontological eliminativism could have well been a much more wide-ranging, appealing and coherently defended view than we are able to witness nowadays. As we have briefly seen in the preceding chapters, in ancient Greek doxography there are detailed accounts showing the conceptual parentage between some, if not all, the Greek philosophers who are the protagonists of this book. Plutarch's *Against Colotes*, Aristocles of Messene's *On Philosophy* as well as Plato's *Theaetetus* (at least on the peirastic interpretation of it that I endorse) are all works of philosophical genealogy that highlight connections and analogies between the doctrines of Protagoras, Pyrrho, the Cyrenaics and Democritus (and, for that matter, Epicurus).

Yet, the focus on those works (let me use this generic term even for the philosophical masterpiece of the *Theaetetus*) is either on the ethical side, with Colotes aiming to show why all philosophers except for the Epicureans make life impossible to live; or it is mainly on epistemological doctrines such as Aristocles' *On Philosophy* or Plato's *Theaetetus*. Ancient philosophers, however, were not strict as we often happen to be nowadays in observing a distinction between different philosophical areas. As we have witnessed in the previous chapters, many metaphysical views that we have been discussing are to be found intersected with relevant discussions on ethical and/or epistemological issues. At the same time, other relevant evidence has been brought in, to paint a fairly detailed and systematic thread of eliminativist arguments in ancient Greek philosophy that for a variety of reasons has so far escaped the attention of scholars.

Together with the reconstruction of the main eliminativist views in ancient Greek philosophy, another salient feature of this book is provided by the comparative effort to relate and compare ancient Greek eliminativism with some Buddhist views that appear to be strikingly similar to the Greek ones. The nature of this comparative effort is mainly theoretical; that is, I have aimed to highlight close conceptual analogies between the ontological doctrines of Gorgias and Nāgārjuna, Protagoras and Vasubandhu, Pyrrho and early Buddhism. By focusing mainly on similarities as well as by highlighting differences in perspective, I claim that by means of a comparative effort such as the one attempted in this book we can gain a better understanding of Greek and Buddhist philosophies, both in themselves and of their dialogical interactions.

Of course, to highlight conceptual analogies can imply that the Western and the Eastern philosophical traditions discovered or developed similar views independently one from the other – as I have argued in Chapter 4 for Pyrrho and Buddhism. Alternatively, one may press the point further from an historical point of view, that is, one may insist on the *too many* analogies that are to be found between Greek and Buddhist philosophies. This would in turn mean that, despite developing different philosophical traditions that have been at least so far kept usually very distinct one from the other, Greek and Buddhist philosophers had the possibility to interact in a profitable way – that is, by means of *historical* connections, influences and encounters. Again, this a philosophy book, or a book that aims to reconstruct an important part of a neglected metaphysical position in the history of thought, both Greek and Buddhist. It is not a history book that is aimed at documenting the historical interactions between Greece and India in the pre-Hellenistic and Hellenistic times. Yet, I suspect that much can be done in this direction, to show how closely interconnected by trade, cultural exchanges, interactions with nomadic people East and West were.[1] Once this ground-breaking work of historical discovery is carried out in its full complexity, we would be in a better position to understand why Greek and Buddhist philosophies show such a degree of conceptual similarities, despite having developed their views within their own, distinct theoretical frameworks.

Eliminativism and indeterminacy

In the book we have seen how Protagoras' Secret Doctrine in the *Theaetetus* provides us with an essential insight into the main features of ontological eliminativism in ancient Greek philosophy. Together with the Heraclitean idea that all is (in) flux and change, the Secret Doctrine is centred on the notion of metaphysical indeterminacy, that is, the view that things in the material world are ontologically indeterminate. Again, this notion of indeterminacy plays an essential role in the sort of metaphysical outlook that one may attribute to Pyrrho in light of a coherent reading of the Aristocles passage (again, with the idea that things are also undifferentiated and, again from an Heraclitean standpoint, unstable). Lastly, the Cyrenaic idea that, at least on my interpretation, material objects are wholly elusive items ultimately rests on metaphysical indeterminacy.

While drawing up a genealogical connection between Protagoras, Pyrrho and the Cyrenaics as eliminativist philosophers endorsing various degrees of metaphysical indeterminacy, in the book it has also been shown that Protagoras' Secret Doctrine has very close conceptual analogies with Vasubandhu's theory of dharmas (Chapter 2) as well as with early Buddhism (Chapter 4). In the latter chapter, in fact, it has been argued not only that Pyrrho's view on things as this has been reconstructed on the basis of Aristocles' passage has close analogies with an essential statement of early Buddhism such as the *Three Characteristics*, but also with the main ontological features displayed by the

Secret Doctrine. This shows that a very detailed parallelism between Greek and Buddhist ontologies is indeed there for us to appreciate.

On the basis of my reconstruction, together with Protagoras, the Cyrenaics, Vasubandhu and early Buddhism, Pyrrho is thus inscribed into a line of ontological thought that is centred on metaphysical indeterminacy. At the same time, at the end of Chapter 4 I have put forward some suggestions on whose basis one may take Pyrrho as closely linked with a nihilist trend in ancient Greek and Buddhist thought whose main figures, again on my interpretation, were Gorgias and Nāgārjuna (and Zeno). After all, Nietzsche calls Pyrrho not only a Buddhist for Greece but also a nihilist.[2] How is it possible, one may now wonder, that Pyrrho is plausibly interpreted as a philosopher whose metaphysical outlook is centred on indeterminacy and, at the same time, as a nihilist philosopher? We have briefly seen in the *Introduction* that eliminativism and nihilism are two distinct views.[3] Is metaphysical indeterminacy (taken as the fundamental view on which ancient eliminativism seems to be grounded) something equivalent to nihilism or indeed as a view ultimately leading to nihilism?

Indeterminacy and nihilism

We may try to answer these questions by looking back again at Pyrrho and at the reception of his thought by later philosophers. While commenting on *Theaetetus* 151e8–152a4, that is, the lines of that dialogue where Protagoras' Maxim that man is the measure of all things is firstly introduced, the Anonymous Commentator on the *Theaetetus* writes:

> The Pyrrhonians say that everything is relative in a different sense, according to which nothing is in itself, but everything is viewed relative to other things. Neither colour nor shape nor sound nor taste nor smells nor textures nor any other object of perception has an intrinsic character on its own–otherwise it would not be possible for the same entities to have different effects according to their distance, or the things seen in combination with them (as when the sea strikes us differently), or the atmospheric conditions (LXIII).

For the Anonymous Commentator, the followers of Pyrrho held the view that nothing is in itself but everything is (seen as) relative to other things. The Pyrrhonians are thus here made to endorse the sort of the metaphysical indeterminacy that we have seen is at the root of Protagoras' Secret Doctrine and, more in general, of ancient eliminativism. The Anonymous Commentator adds a further explanation to show what metaphysical indeterminacy really amounts to. He says that 'neither colour nor shape nor sound nor taste nor smells nor textures nor any other object of perception has an intrinsic character on its own'. That is, since they lack what Buddhist thinkers such as Nāgārjuna would call 'intrinsic essence or nature' (*svabhāva*),[4] material objects are best seen as metaphysically indeterminate. On the basis of the Anonymous Commentator's argument, the lack of intrinsic essence and metaphysical indeterminacy are two closely connected views, so that one implies the other.

What is really striking here is that very similar words to the ones employed by the Anonymous Commentator to describe the views of the Pyrrhonians are used in one of the most celebrated texts of Buddhism, the *Heart Sutra*.[5] Here is the passage I am referring to in the graceful translation by Alex Kerr:

> Therefore, within this emptiness,
> There is no material world.
> There is no sensation, Thought,
> Action or Consciousness.
> No eyes, ears, nose tongue, body
> Or mind.
> No colour, sound, scent, taste,
> Touch or dharmas. (Part 4 in Kerr's edition)

Kerr's comment on this part of the *Heart Sutra* is particularly illuminating. Let me quote part of it. Kerr writes:

> From here on, the sutra takes up each aspect of how we view and live in the world, one at a time, and negates them all. This may be the most 'negating' piece of writing in human history [...]. The sutra turns out the lights and shuts down the music, stating simply and soberly: 'There is no material world'. The next lines go on to cut away the means by which we apprehend reality, including the sense organs (eyes, nose, etc.) and the senses associated with them: 'colour' (standing for sight), sound and so forth. All these things are illusions. (Kerr 2022, pp. 104–5)

Two things need highlighting here. As for the first, the *Heart Sutra*, the most popular sutra in Mahayana Buddhism, relies heavily on ideas famously developed by Nāgārjuna, among which the notion of emptiness features prominently.[6] In Chapter 3, I have made a case for interpreting Nāgārjuna's philosophy of emptiness as possibly leading to nihilism, inviting readers and scholars alike to revise more traditional hermeneutical interpretations. The section of the *Heart Sutra* just quoted seems to make emptiness eventually collapse into nihilism, since 'within this emptiness' there seems to be really nothing: no material world, no sensation, no thought, no action and so on.

As for the second point I wish to highlight, when the section of the *Heart Sutra* quoted above is read in parallel with the passage taken from the Anonymous Commentator on the *Theaetetus*, a revealing point is made. When he refers to the followers of Pyrrho, the Anonymous Commentator mentions metaphysical indeterminacy, while explaining it further with a reference to the lack of intrinsic existence of material things. Since 'colour nor shape nor sound nor taste nor smells nor textures nor any other object of perception has an intrinsic character on its own', that is, since they lack intrinsic essence, material things are ontologically indeterminate.

As seen, these words of the Anonymous Commentator are echoed in the *Heart Sutra*, where it is said that 'within this emptiness, there is no material world. There is no sensation, Thought, Action or Consciousness. No eyes, ears, nose tongue, body or mind. No colour, sound, scent, taste, Touch or dharma'. But as just noted, behind the emptiness of the *Heart Sutra* nihilism appears to step in as the ultimately true view of the material world. This may well be the case too if we look closer at what the Anonymous Commentator says on the Pyrrhonians. If we stretch indeterminacy at a higher, or perhaps lower, level, we end up in thinking that behind the view that things are ontologically indeterminate there is, more fundamentally, the idea that nothing really is (anything). Since nothing is really ontologically determinate in one way or another, well, nothing is intrinsically anything. Nothing thus is. Nihilism can be the more radical metaphysical ground on which indeterminacy rests. That is why Pyrrho can be consistently seen as an indeterminist and a nihilist thinker.

This is one interpretative explanation of the conceptual connection between ontological eliminativism, indeterminacy and nihilism that was drawn in ancient philosophy by such sources as the Anonymous Commentator. It is exactly because of this connection, which I think is well founded from a conceptual point of view, that I have included the discussion of Gorgias and Nāgārjuna in this book. The sort of nihilist arguments put forward by both

Gorgias and Nāgārjuna, at least on the interpretation that I recommend, is an integral part of a more general eliminativist trend in ancient philosophy that from Protagoras, Gorgias and the Cyrenaics, through Pyrrho, is deeply connected with a similar line of thought that is reflected in some of Vasubandhu's and Nāgārjuna's views.

Invoking some sort of theoretical inaccuracy, a contemporary reader may protest that the lack of any distinction between eliminativism, indeterminacy and nihilism is a bad move for ancient philosophers because, although the three views are also closely interrelated, they are also distinct positions. Yet, the close parentage between indeterminacy (and eliminativism) on the one hand and nihilism on the other appears to be wholly present in the contemporary metaphysical debate too. When the option of radical indeterminacy (that is, the idea prominent in Protagoras' Secret Doctrine that that things are ontologically indeterminate in all respects)[7] is joined with stuff ontology (that is, with the idea that ultimately there is a material stuff where indeterminacy takes place),[8] we obtain ontological eliminativism. The world is ontologically indeterminate, but there is some grounding for such an indeterminate reality – so material objects are eliminated, but there is something, there is an indeterminate reality.

On the contrary, when radical indeterminacy is not paired with stuff ontology but with the idea that it is dependence all the way down with no real matter to rely on,[9] we get nihilism. If things are ontologically indeterminate in all respects and if indeterminacy is a matter of ontological dependence with no ultimate, final ground where to start or stop the grounding process, nihilism will be the most likely metaphysical option to adopt. It is just a matter of degrees if we want to separate eliminativism, indeterminacy and nihilism in more fundamental and meaningful ways. This is the case in both ancient and contemporary debates.

Notes

Introduction

1 This is different from the sort of eliminativism (or eliminative materialism) about mental states that is one of the main views to be debated in contemporary philosophy of mind. On this view, see the useful entry in the Stanford Encyclopaedia of Philosophy: Ramsey, William, 'Eliminative Materialism', *The Stanford Encyclopedia of Philosophy* (Spring 2022 edition), Edward N. Zalta (ed.), https://plato.stanford.edu/archives/spr2022/entries/materialism-eliminative/.

2 On Pyrrho and nihilism, see the Conclusion.

3 Aristocle of Messene is a Peripatetic philosopher whose work *On Philosophy* is an important source for reconstructing the views of those ancient Greek philosophers who are the protagonists of this book, especially Pyrrho (see chapter 4 on the scholarly debate surrounding the so-called Aristocles passage). Aristocles' original work is lost and is partially preserved in the work of Eusebius of Caesarea. Chiesara (2001) is a very useful reconstruction of Aristocles' *On Philosophy*, with a detailed commentary (F4 on Pyrrho, F5 on the Cyrenaics, F6 on Protagoras).

Plutarch's *Against Colotes* reconstructs some of the main arguments contained in Colotes' original work *On the fact that according to the doctrines of other philosophers it is impossible even to live*. Kechagia (2011) provides a systematic analysis of Colotes' main philosophical points as well as of Plutarch's own arguments against him. Colotes' work as preserved and commented on by Plutarch is a fundamental source for reconstructing Cyrenaic views (and Democritus'): see Plutarch, *Against Colotes* 1120c–1121e. On *Against Colotes*, see also Corti (2014).

Diogenes Laertius' *On the Lives of Eminent Philosophers* is a doxographical source on the lives and thought of all major and minor Greek philosophers. Protagoras and Pyrrho are dealt with in Book 9 while Aristippus and the Cyrenaics are to be found in Book 2. Notoriously difficult to edit, Dorandi (2013) is an excellent new edition of Diogenes' *Lives*.

4 The task of attributing a clear metaphysical commitment to both Gorgias and the Cyrenaics requires a more careful work than what has so far been attempted. I try to do this in chapters 3, 5 and 6.

5   Van Inwagen (1990) defends eliminativism about material objects by rejecting the actual possibility of material composition (what he calls the 'Special Composition Question'). Merricks (2001) on the other hand argues for eliminating material objects on the basis of the argument that material objects have no causal role over and above the causal role of their microphysical parts. Although for different theoretical reasons, both Van Inwagen and Merricks make exception for the actual existence of living organisms. Benovsky (2018) is a sophisticated attempt to argue for the virtue of non-existence of both objects and people, drawing inspirations from some seminal papers by Peter Unger (such as Unger 1979a and Unger 1979b) and from Buddhist philosophy.

6   See Westerhoff (2020a) and (2020b). While drawing its true inspirations from his wide knowledge of Buddhist philosophy (especially Nāgārjuna's) and at the same time employing the richness of the theoretical apparatus of analytic philosophy, Westerhoff (2020b) is an extremely ambitious and sophisticated attempt to argue for the non-existence of the external and internal worlds, as well as of any ontological foundations and foundational truths. Rightly, Westerhoff insists on the conceptual distinction between (ontological) eliminativism and nihilism. It is the combination between eliminativism (that is, the view that there are no material objects and/or selves) and non-foundationalism (it is dependence all the way down) that generates nihilism. I further comment on eliminativism and nihilism in the Conclusion. There are also two other works by contemporary metaphysicians dealing with nothingness, that is, Sorensen (2022) and Mumford (2021). Both have some sections on ancient nihilism, especially Sorensen: on Gorgias (p. 105), on the Buddha (pp. 38–61), on Nāgārjuna (pp. 63–76).

7   It is worth highlighting that we are here talking about philosophers who we may perceive, from our distorted perspective, as minor but who were not understood as secondary figures by their contemporaries or, more generally, in antiquity. Protagoras and Gorgias were two leading sophists whose views received close scrutiny by Plato (mainly in the *Theaetetus*, as we shall see, but also in the *Protagoras*, in the *Cratylus* and, again at a lesser extent, in the *Gorgias*) and Aristotle (especially in his discussion on the Principle of non-contradiction in Book Gamma of the *Metaphysics*). The Cyrenaics – that is, philosophers from Cyrene, the so-called Athens of Africa for its wealth, cultural effervescence and historical relevance – were an important Socratic and post-Socratic school that spanned over three centuries, developing a form of hedonism that firstly preceded-and then contrasted with – the more celebrated hedonism of the Epicureans. Lastly, Pyrrho. Despite the really meagre evidence on him and his thought (see chapter 4), Pyrrho was recognized as the founder of (Pyrrhonian)

scepticism and, hence, given enormous importance in the history of Greek philosophy.

On Protagoras, see Zilioli (2007, reprinted 2016), Corradi (2012); on Gorgias, see Mazzara (1999), Ioli (2013) and Di Iulio (2022); on the Cyrenaics, see Tsouna (1998), Zilioli (2012), Lampe (2014a); on Pyrrho, see Bett (2000).

8 See Sorensen (2022, pp. 102–18), on ancient atomism and nothingness.
9 See e.g. Pasnau (2007) and Kechagia (2011, pp. 180–7, 193–200).
10 Plutarch's *Against Colotes*, 1111b–f and Kechagia (2011, pp. 201–12).
11 The main reasons for which I have not been able to include Democritus in the discussion of eliminativism this book is centred on are mainly two. The first, less essential, is that both Pasnau and Kechagia have done much to show that Democritean eliminativism is a plausible scholarly reading of ancient atomism. The second reason, more fundamental, is that to deal with Democritean eliminativism implies opening up a trend of issues and topics that would require a book in itself. These topics, which would have required at least four chapters in this book, would include (1) the relation between Democritean and Epicurean atomism (Is Plutarch right in equating Democritean eliminativist atomism with Epicurus'?); (2) the question of whether ancient atomist eliminativism concerns persons too. There is a huge debate on Epicurean selfhood on which much has been written: see the seminal papers by Sedley (Sedley 1983 and 1988), the response to Sedley's claims by O'Keefe (O'Keefe 2005) and the more recent appraisal by Nemeth (2017); (3) the analogies and differences between ancient Greek and Buddhist atomisms, on which recently see Carpenter (2020) and (2023). Similar remarks apply to Heraclitus. The infamous obscurity of his philosophy, together with close analogies that his philosophy seem to have with Buddhism (see e.g. McEvilley 2002, pp. 430–2) asks for a full, substantial treatment in itself.
12 See Gill (2006), Sorabji (2006). More recently, see Nemeth (2017).
13 See Parfit (1987, part III). As for the Cyrenaics, it has been traditionally believed that they endorsed a traditional, all-or-nothing conception of selfhood (see Tsouna 1998, pp. 131–4). I have challenged this interpretation in Zilioli (2012, pp. 111–19), again by relying on Parfit's insights into personal reductionism and while following the attempt of Terry Irwin (Irwin 1991).
14 See Parfit (1987, pp. 202–9; 214–17).
15 Parfit's treatment of selfhood and personal identity was indeed innovative, since he does consciously shape his philosophy as 'revisionary', not 'descriptive' (Parfit 1987, p. X).
16 Both works, together with excellent commentaries, are translated by James Duerlinger (see respectively Duerlinger 2003, 2013). On the Personalists as

defending a non-reductionist theory of persons, see Priestley (1999), Carpenter (2015) and Westerhoff (2018, pp. 163–8).

17 Dharmakīrti *The Proof of the Existence of Other Minds* and Ratnakīrti's *The Refutation of the Existence of Other Minds* may well be in read in parallel, to show how developed the Buddhist debate on other minds was. A good introduction to such a debate is Wood (1991).

18 Among the Greek philosophers who are the protagonists of this book, that is, Protagoras, Gorgias, Pyrrho and the Cyrenaics themselves, the latter are the ones who are credited to have discovered the very notion of 'subjectivity' in the ancient world. This is the main point made in three different articles by Gail Fine (2003a, 2003b, 2004), who challenges the argument against idealism put forward by Burnyeat (in Burnyeat 1982). On the Burnyeat/Fine debate on idealism and subjectivity, see Gill (2006, section 6.6).

19 See McEvilley (2002).

20 See Stoneman (2019). I get back to this point in the Conclusion.

21 See recently, e.g., Seaford (2017) and Gowans (2021).

22 See Zilioli (2012).

Chapter 1

1 See Chappell (2020) for an ingenious interpretation of the overall dialectic strategy put in place by Socrates in the *Theaetetus*, for which the dialogue is in fact not-aporetic.

2 As for the *Theaetetus*, I mainly use the translation by Christopher Rowe (Rowe 2015b).

3 For a reconstruction of Protagoras' views in Plato, see Zilioli (2007); for an exhaustive treatment of Protagoras in Aristotle's works, both in philosophical and in historical terms, with full reference to the extensive scholarship on the topic, see Corradi (2012).

4 I have addressed the problem in Zilioli (2007).

5 *Tht.* 152c10: 'Has he given us this as a riddle for the common riff-raff, while revealing the Truth to his disciples in secret? (*tois de mathêtais en aporrêtôi tên alêtheian elegen*)'.

6 For strong and mild indeterminacy, see Rosen/Smith (2004) and *Oxford Studies in Metaphysics* 6 (2011), with chapters by E. Barnes and R. Williams (*A Theory of Metaphysical Indeterminacy*), M. Eklund (*Being Metaphysically*

Unsettled) and R. Woodward (*Metaphysical Indeterminacy and Vague Existence*). See also chapter 4, pp. 79–81 and chapter 5, pp. 87–8.

7   See *Tht.* 157c1-2, and pp. 24–7, section 4.

8   There is here a close parallelism to be drawn between the problem of reference as raised in Protagoras' Secret Doctrine and similar problems raised by Socrates' Dream in the last part of the dialogue, on which see recently Chappell (2020). Again, I don't think that this parallelism has been investigated with the attention it does deserve. See Sedley (2004, pp. 150–68) for the suggestion that Parts I and III of the *Theaetetus* are more linked that what it appears at first sight.

9   I need to praise Rowe's translation here. He ameliorates the Levett/Burnyeat's on a crucial point; at *Tht.* 154 a2 the expression (as referred to colour) '*alla metaxu ti hekastôi idion gegonos*' is to be translated as 'something that has come to be in between the two, peculiar to each one' (that is, to the percipient and the perceived object), and not as 'something which has come into being between the two, and which is private to the individual percipient', a translation that obliterates the correlativity that is at the root of the theory of perception Socrates is illustrating.

10 Much has been written on these thinkers, myself arguing that they are likely to be Aristippus and the early Cyrenaics: Zilioli (2013a). I believe a serious case can be made to show that Plato thinks the Cyrenaics as Protagoras' best heirs at his (Plato's) time. Tsouna provides the best case I am aware of to deny this identification: Tsouna (1998, Chapter 10); Rowe adopts a third way to the extent that he bypasses the problem of the identity of the subtler thinkers while suggesting that there are surely Cyrenaic traces in the *Theaetetus*: Rowe (2015a).

11 'So Theaetetus, what is this story telling us, in relation to what we were saying before? … Well, see if we can somehow round the story off' (*Tht.* 156c7-8).

12 Socrates to Theaetetus: 'In that case it was quite right for you to say that knowledge was nothing else but perception. Everything has come together – the view of Homer and Heraclitus and the whole of that sort of tribe, that all things change like rivers; that idea of Protagoras, too, paragon of wisdom, that the measure of all things is a human being; and now Theaetetus' proposal, that if all that is so, perception turns out to be knowledge. How about it, Theaetetus? Shall we claim this as your new-born baby, as it were, delivered by me as midwife?' (*Tht.* 160d5-e4).

13 Burnyeat (1990, pp. 7–10).

14 Socrates' refutation of Heracliteanism ideally takes place at *Tht.* 181b-183c. This is roughly Socrates' argument there: if it were true that everything is always changing in all respects (that is, by changing location through movement as well as altering qualitatively), it would be impossible to say something meaningful at

all, since we could not even name objects in the world. Two things to note. The first is that this is a tentative refutation of *one aspect* of the Secret Doctrine, that is, flux; it is not even an attempt to refute the sort of ontological indeterminacy that is one of the other major elements on which the Secret Doctrine is built. Secondly, Socrates' argument does not seem to be a strong one. Language, and for that matter thought as expressible in language, is perfectly possible even when language is not referential. Something similar to Socrates' argument against Heracliteanism (but see my note 18, p. 144) may be retorted against Pyrrho on language (see chapter 4, pp. 72–4): again, this does not seem to be problematic there. Pyrrho chooses not to speak the conventional language but this does not mean that he is in an absurd position. Closer to us in time, the only attempt to show that the Secret Doctrine *as a whole* is refuted in the *Theaetetus* is Buckels (2016). I take issue with Buckels' interpretation in the following chapter.

15   See above, note 10, p. 130.
16   See Ademollo (2007) and Campbell (1861, pp. XXX–XXXIV).
17   I take up Bett's suggestion in chapter 4, where, while agreeing with Bett on the metaphysical interpretation of Pyrrho's thought, I disagree with him as far as the origin and genealogy of Pyrrhonism are concerned.

Chapter 2

1   See Stage Two explanation in Chapter 1, especially the 'A new theory of perception: Stage Two (the Subtler Thinkers: Theaet. 156a–157c)' section (Chapter 1, pp. 20–4).
2   The identity of Vasubandhu, one of the greatest Buddhist philosphers, is still disputed. Since there is an apparent clash between some of the views that are usually attributed to him (some sounding traditionally as those of an Abhidharma scholar, while other views are typically those of a Yogācārin), Frauwallner (1951) has postulated the existence of two Vasubandhuses. For some difficulties about this hypothesis, see Westerhoff (2018, pp. 158–60).
3   *Tht.* 157a3–9.
4   See above, Chapter 1, pp. 24–5.
5   See also Burnyeat (1990, p. 19)/Buckels (2016, p. 281).
6   See Burnyeat (1990, p. 16) and Buckels (2016, p. 247). In his categorization, Buckels relies on previous efforts by Day (1997).
7   See Day (1997, p. 57).
8   Sedley (2005, p. 46).

9   Buckles (2016, p. 256).
10 Buckels (2016, p. 257).
11 Buckles (2016, p. 258).
12 Buckles (2016, p. 258).
13 See Ronkin (2005) for an helpful introduction to early Buddhist metaphysics.
14 On the Abhidharma schools, see Westerhoff (2018, pp. 35–83). All quotations in this chapter from Vasubandhu are taken from the *Abhidharmakośa*, so I shall give only references to chapters and sections. The translation I use is the standard one by Leo Pruden (Berkeley: Asian Humanities Press, 1988), which is an English translation from the French of Louis de la Vallée Poussin (1923–31), who translated from the Sanskrit text.
15 See 1.20a–b.
16 I give the full passage of *Abhidharmakośa* 1.43d where Vasubandhu's argument is put forward in the new translation by Carpenter/Ngaserin (in Zilioli 2020, pp. 172–3):

   That means that they attain their objects. In the case of smell, how is it that the object is attained? Because there is no grasping of an odour when there is no breathing in. What is this term 'attain'? Occurring without interval. (3) But do atoms touch one another or not? (4) The Kaśmīris say, 'they do not touch'. What is the reason? If they were to touch completely, things would coalesce. Then suppose instead that they were to touch at one spot. There would be the unwanted result that they have parts – and atoms do not have parts. (5) Then how is there the production of sound? For that very reason. For if they were to touch, a hand that strikes at a hand, a rock that strikes at a rock, would become attached. (6) How does a heap that is struck not break apart? Because it is in a state of being held together by the air element (*vāyu-dhātu*). A certain air element acts for the purpose of scattering, just as in the destruction of the world; a certain one for the purpose of holding together, just as in the creation of the world. (7) How in this case can it be said that the three [organs] attain their object by reaching without interval? There not being anything in the middle is indeed a state of non-interval for these [organs]. (8) Moreover, the statement that 'agglomerations touch because they have parts' is without error. (9) And supposing thus, this section in the *Vibhāṣā* is correct: Having asked the question 'Now does a thing-in-contact arise caused by a thing-in – contact or caused by a thing-not-in-contact?', it then answers: 'It depends on the cause. Sometimes, a thing-not-in-contact arises caused by a thing-in-contact when it breaks. Sometimes a thing-in-contact is caused by a thing-not-in-contact when it goes to a heap. Sometimes a thing-in-contact is caused by a thing-in-contact when heaps are combined. Sometimes a thing-not-in-contact is caused by a thing-not-in – contact, as when dust stays in the air'. (10) Bhadanta Vasumitra says, 'if atoms were to touch, they would stay a moment later'. Bhadanta says, 'they do not touch; but there is a cognition of touch when they are without interval'. And the opinion of Bhadanta ought to be accepted. (11) For otherwise, were atoms to have space in between them, by what would their going into the empty intervals be restrained? For atoms need to have resistance. (12) And it is not the case that agglomerations are anything other than atoms. Those very things (i.e., atoms) can be made an object of touch insofar as they are agglomerations, just as they can be made an object of perception. (13) And regarding atoms: if division according to directions is being supposed, then there is the unwanted result that they have parts – whether they touch or not. If not supposed, then even when they do touch, there is no unwanted result.

In Carpenter (2020), Carpenter offers an ingenious solutions to the Problems of Contact and Agglomeration that are typically held to trouble Vasubandhu's 'physical' atomism, thus arguing for a possible commitment by him to a large scale atomism that is more radical and appealing than Democritus'. On a similar argument made by Nāgārjuna against atomism, see Chapter 3, the 'Nāgārjuna's argument against change', pp. 57–9.

17 See Carpenter (2020, p. 161).
18 For a very useful overview of the meaning of dharma in Buddhist philosophy, see Warder (1971), which relies on – and provides some criticism of – Stcherbatsky (1922).
19 Stcherbatsky (1922, p. 75); see also Warder (1971, p. 273).
20 Stcherbatsky adds a fourth element, that '*nirvāna* alone is *çānta*', that is, 'the final suppression is the only Calm' (Stcherbatsky 1922, p. 25), thus distinguishing the Tibetan tradition that allows for four marks (or seals) of existence from the Southerner traditions, which allows for three (possibly subsuming the fourth into *duhkha*).
21 See Stcherbatsky (1922), pp. 26–7.
22 On instability, impermanence and momentariness, see Von Rospatt (1995), mainly covering the field up to Vasubandhu, and Feldman and Philips (2011, on Ratnakīrti) and Kim (1999, on Theravāda).
23 See Stcherbatsky (1922, pp. 37–8).
24 Westerhoff (2018, p. 75).
25 See Stcherbatsky (1922, p. 6). Against this, see Goodman (2004, pp. 396–7) and Warder (1971, pp. 273–4).
26 On dharmas as tropes, see Carpenter (2014, pp. 44–5), Goodman (2004). On the genealogy of tropes in contemporary metaphysics, see Simons (2020), which conceives of the ontology of tropes as the only form of atomism 'worth having'.

27 See e.g. Bareau (2013, p. 208), Kritzer (2003, p. 206).
28 See pp. 33–4.
29 See Buckles (2016, p. 259), p. 36.
30 On supervenience, a fundamental concept in contemporary analytic philosophy, see the very useful entry by B. McLaughlin and K. Bennett in the *Stanford Encyclopaedia of Philosophy*, https://plato.stanford.edu/archives/sum2021/entries/supervenience/), especially the 'Supervenience, Grounding, and Ontological Dependence' section on supervenient, grounding and ontological dependence. See also Lewis (1999) and Kim (1993).
31 Vasubandhu classifies all dharmas into five groups: matter (*rūpa*); feelings (*vedanā*), ideas (*samjñā*), volitions (*samskāra*) and consciousness (*vijñāna*). See Stcherbastky (1922, pp. 6/7).
32 See *Abhidharmakośa* 2.22 and Carpenter (2020).
33 See *Abhidharmakośa* 1.13 and Goodman (2004).
34 While commenting on this passage, Goodman writes, 'the claim that the great elements sustain derived form must ultimately mean that tropes of derived form are being brought into existence every moment as long as new tropes of the great elements continue arising to create them' (Goodman 2004, p. 398).

Chapter 3

1 As far as I am aware, there is only a brief account (one page) on Gorgias and Mādhyamika in McEvilley (2002, pp. 427–8). McEvilley's interpretation is very different from the one argued for in this chapter: see the 'Retrospect and conclusion' section.
2 I champion Di Iulio (2021) as the most recent attempt to discharge Gorgias' nihilism as a serious philosophical position. Alternatively, see Sedley (2017, especially pp. 5–6, 17, 24–5) for an interesting attempt to take Zeno and Gorgias as thinkers endorsing nihilism. On Gorgias as mainly a rhetor, see Wardy (1996, especially part I).
3 See the 'Nāgārjuna and nihilism' section below, pp. 54ff.
4 Metaphysical nihilism is a view that has recently got some tracking in analytic philosophy: see e.g. Turner (2011), Benovsky (2019) and Westerhoff (2020a). Westerhoff takes metaphysical nihilism as the combination of ontological eliminativism (as he puts it, 'only the fundamental exists', 2020a, p. 1) and

non-foundationalism ('it's dependence all the way down', ibidem). See also Introduction, p. 127, note 6.

5   Sedley (2017, p. 24) suggests with good reasons Eudemus of Rhodes as the possible author of MXG exactly in light of the nihilist lineage in ancient thought that the MXG seems to be addressing.

6   See Ioli (2010). Since Ioli's edition provides an Italian translation of Gorgias' treatise, I shall use the English translation of PTMO that Laks and Most have prepared in their 2016 Loeb Collection (Early Greek Philosophy. Sophists. Part 1, vol. VIII, pp. 218–25, henceforth LM). I will rely on Ioli's own English translation for those key passages of Gorgias' dialectical logos that as a locus deperditus Laks and Most do not translate (see Ioli 2021).

7   See MXG 979a11–13 and S.E., M. 7.65.

8   The fact that Sextus uses the trilemma in his presentation of Gorgias' arguments has often been taken as evidence that he moulded Gorgias' original arguments into the favourite sceptical way of argumentation, thus distorting Gorgias' original views. On the basis of this argument, the Anonymous' version has been preferred, because it was allegedly closer to Gorgias' PTMO. This view has been recently challenged by Rodriguez (2019). I am not going to address the long-standing dispute about which is to be preferred between the two accounts of Gorgias' PTMO, since it is the actual combination of them that allows us to get a good understanding of Gorgias' views (see Bett 2020, pp. 190–4).

9   Following Ioli (2021, p. 6, note 2), I replace the LM translation: 'the unlimited could not ever be' with 'the unlimited could not be anywhere'.

10 Following Ioli (2021, p. 8, note 7), I replace the LM translation: 'and certainly it could not come to be from what is either' with the more cogent: 'Nor certainly could it come to be from what is not'.

11 21 D2 LM. It is worth highlighting that in the reconstruction of Gorgias' arguments in the dialectical logos some references to other arguments originally put forward by Zeno and Melissus are often made. In the context of the present chapter, it is impossible, if not only briefly, to show how Gorgias originally modified or indeed reinvented Eleatic arguments for his own philosophical scopes: on the topic, see Rossetti (2017) and Ioli (2021). On Zeno and Nāgārjunā, see also McEvilley (2002, pp. 422–6).

12 21 D3–5 LM.

13 21 D6 LM.

14 We don't know much about Zeno's argument about place (see 20 D 13a&b LM), which seems to be closely related to his famous argument against

motion (20 D17 LM; see also 20 D14,15, 16, 18 and 19LM). Relying on Eudemus of Rhodes' reconstruction (to be found in Simplicius), Sedley has thus reconstructed and widened Zeno's argument on place along nihilist lines that are very suitable for Gorgias' move here. Here is Sedley's reconstruction: 'Since whatever exists must be in a place, if place itself existed it would be in a place, and that place in a further place, and so on and so forth, which is absurd. Therefore place does not exist. But if anything existed it would be in a place. Therefore nothing exists' (Sedley 2017, pp. 23/4; see also p. 25).

15 See 21 D8 LM, adding 'and if it had thickness, it would have parts, and would no longer be one' as the final line of the fragment, which is missing in LM. The attribution to Melissus of this fragment is still dubious, some claiming that it could reflect Zeno's views (see Palmer 2003).
16 20 D5 LM.
17 Bett (2020, p. 194) writes that 'one could also regard the argument against motion as an additional element in the case its being one or many'. This is certainly the case; yet the two arguments against motion that Gorgias is reported to have used in his dialectical logos do have a philosophical life on their own.
18 This argument rests on the Eleatic assumption that being is fully and completely homogeneous, that is, always identical to itself and undergoing no ontological change whatsoever. On Melissus and being as homogeneous, see 21 D19 LM (=MXG 974a12-14).
19 On Melissus on motion and divisibility, see 21 D9 LM.
20 On which, see Ioli (2021), Sattler (2020); below, pp. 59–61.
21 See Westerhoff (2018, pp. 89–146) for the main tenets and figures of the Madhyamaka school.
22 See Garfield (1996), Burton (2014, pp. 19–44).
23 See e.g., MMK (=*Mūlamadhymakakārikā*) 15:6–11, 24:18a–b. See also, below, pp. 56–7, 'the Nāgārjuna's Argument against Eternalism' section.
24 See e.g., VV (=*Vigrahavyāvartanī*) 11–12, 61–4 and ŚS 15 (spoken by an opponent). For Nāgārjuna as denying any commitment to nihilism, see e.g., MMK 5:6–8, 8:12–13, 15:6–7.
25 See e.g., MMK 24:7, 36.
26 See mainly Wood (1994), Tola and Dragonetti (1995), Burton (2014), Westerhoff (2009) and (2016, with a full sketch on the nihilistic interpretations of Nāgārjuna in the history of thought).
27 Burton (1994, p. 88). Some passages of the MMK can indeed be read as pointing towards nihilism: see 15:1–4, 5:5, 23:8; see also ŚS 58 and 67. On Nāgārjuna

as a philosopher well aware of the kind of nihilism that is implicit in his theory of emptiness, see Wood (1994); on Nāgārjuna as unaware of this, see Burton (1994).

28 For MMK, I mainly rely on the excellent translation by Mark Siderits and Shōryū Katsura (2013).

29 For ŚS, I usually rely on the transition of either Tola and Dragonetti (1995) or Lindtner (1987), which remains fundamental for a detailed overview of all the works by Nāgārjuna (with very useful notes on editions and manuscripts).

30 I take all these works to be genuine works by Nāgārjuna: on the question of authenticity, see Lindtner (1987).

31 On the Abhidharma schools, see Westerhoff (2018, pp. 35–83); on the notion of *svabhāva* as substance, see Westerhoff (2009, pp. 29–40); Burton (2014, pp. 90-4 and 213-20). The Sanskrit term '*svabhāva*' is a compound term, with '*sva*' meaning 'one's own' or 'oneself' and '*bhāva*' referring to a thing, the actual nature of a thing or, more generally, to the existence of a thing. The idea behind all this is that to exist, a thing must have 'bhāva' on its own, that is, without depending ontologically on anything else.

32 It is true that the generation and causation are two different concepts, but I also believe that it can be argued that what 'generation' does in the philosophical arguments of the PTMO can be well compared to what 'causation' does in Nāgārjuna's works. I am also ready to admit that the role Nāgārjuna gives to causation in his philosophy is much greater than the one Gorgias gives to generation in the PTMO; yet this does not prevent us from comparing the two ideas fruitfully, at least in the context of the kind of comparison I am drawing in this chapter.

33 On causation as conceptually constructed for Nāgārjuna, see Siderits (2004). See also Garfield (1994, 2001).

34 See also MMK 1:10, 24:16, ŚS 3-5.

35 On Nāgārjuna's use of the tetralemma, see Westerhoff (2009, chapter 4).

36 See the whole of MMK 1.

37 On Nagarjuna advocating the emptiness of all dharmas as the true middle path, see MMK 21: 13&14, 15:7.

38 For Abhidharmikas, the dispute between eternalism and annihilationism mainly concerns persons and selves, while Nāgārjuna widens it to material things too: see Siderits and Katsura (2013, pp. 203–5, 235–9).

39 For example, MMK 17:10, 18:10.

40 See the Argument against Change section below, pp. 55–9.

41 See Siderits (2016, pp. 28–30).
42 On the One-Many argument in both Ancient Greek philosophy and Buddhism, see McEvilley (2002, chapter 2).
43 See also ŚS 7.
44 On this argument, see Carpenter (2020), with an Appendix offering a fresh translation on the relevant passage from *Abhidharmakośabhāsya*. See also Kapstein (2001), Tola and Dragonetti (2004, pp. 127–9, 142–5) (where the relevant stanzas and sections of Vasubandhu's *Twenty Verses* are translated and commented on).
45 Similar argument against atomism and partless entities are to be found in a short treatise, likely to be by Nāgārjuna's disciple, Āryadeva, which often goes under the Tibetan title of *Treatise on the division of parts*: see Tola and Dragonetti (1995, pp. 1–17, especially pp. 11–13).
46 See also MMK 13: 1&2.
47 See also MMK 23:24, 21:17.
48 See, respectively, Siderits and O'Brien (1976), Mabbett (1984) and Galloway (1987) for the first kind of reading and Westerhoff (2008, 2009, chapter 4) for the second reading. More recently, see Arnold (2012).
49 This chapter falls short of any pretence about historical transmission. Much has been done in recent years to show that East and West were much linked that we thought of decades ago – and this is especially true when we refer to Greek and Buddhist thought: for a start, see McEvilley (2002, chapters 1, 14 and all the four Appendixes) and Stoneman (2021); see also Beckwith (2015) and Halkias (2014) on Pyrrho and the Buddhists. But to speculate on the possible ways Gorgias' arguments may have reached East goes well beyond this chapter's limits. On the point, see McEvilley (2002, chapter 18).
50 For a reading of Nāgārjuna's philosophy as mainly sceptical or dialectical, see Burton (1999, part I) and McEvilley (2002, chapters 17 and 18). On the main reasons for which the sceptical reading is to be refuted, see Burton (1999, pp. 30–44).
51 See *Vigrahavyāvartanī* 24 (on which see Westerhoff 2010, p. 54, which refers to similar charges brought against global relativism and anti-realism by Paul Boghossian).
52 I shall further comment on indeterminacy and nihilism in the Conclusion.
53 Nietzsche, *The Will to Power*, Book 2, section 437 (on which see Bett 2000a).
54 See Beckwith (2015, p. 29) and chapter 4, p. 76.
55 As Tola and Dragonetti put it: 'Even if the Mādhyamika does not affirm nothingness, anyhow its conception of reality as "void", the emphasis it lays on

universal contingency, the affirmation of the unreality of all and the analytical-abolishing method in order to reach truth, have led us to the conclusion that the Mādhyamika philosophy represents the most radical degree of philosophical nihilism' (Tola and Dragonetti 1995, *Preface*).

Chapter 4

1   On the reasons why Timon is a reliable source, see Decleva Caizzi (1981, pp. 220–2), Bett (1994), Bett (2000, pp. 16–18). More balanced is the judgement by Chiesara (2001, pp. 91 and 99). *Contra*, see Brunschwig (1994) and note 4. For Decleva Caizzi's critical edition of Pyrrho, I use the classical 1981 edition; there is also a new reprint of this edition, together with an English translation of Pyrrho's sources (by M. Bonazzi and D. Sedley) and some other essays by Decleva Caizzi herself on Pyrrho and scepticism: Decleva Caizzi (2020).

2   Despite the abundant literature on it, little has been said on the style of Pyrrho's Questions&Answers in the Aristocles passage. As already highlighted, the logic of the passage is stringent; yet Pyrrho's answers to the original questions are perceived as hieratically given, with no further arguments to support them. It is as if Pyrrho's knowledge (about the nature of things, the way we should be disposed towards them and the practical conduct to adopt) is a sort of pre-philosophical wisdom that he offers to those who come to him: see Ferrari (1981, pp. 350–1). The sacerdotal aspect of Pyrrho's approach helps us understand supernatural, almost divine nature that in his portrait Timon recognizes to Pyrrho: see e.g., fr. 67 Diels, vv 5–8. Similarities between the divine Pyrrho and the Buddha can here be drawn too: see Nietzsche, *The Will to Power*, book 2, section 437; see also Chapter 3, the 'Retrospect and conclusion' section.

3   All the three adjectives begin with a privative alpha, meaning that the outlook about things to be gained is a negative one, since all the three adjectives point at some features of things lacking in some way or another. I take the reference to '*ep'isēs*' as simply 'equally', to mean emphasis: as Bett puts it, 'all three of the epithets used to describe things apply to all things equally – that is, […] things are every bit as indifferent, as they are unstable and indeterminate' (Bett 2000, p. 28); *contra*, see Decleva Caizzi (1981, p. 223).

   '*Adiáphora*' means 'without any difference between things', which again, can be read ontologically (that is, 'things in themselves have no ontological difference') or epistemologically (that is, 'things have no logical differentiations between themselves because we are unable to differentiate them'). To support her metaphysical reading, Decleva Caizzi points out some similar passages by Aristotle (in *M.* 4.1007b25–7; 1008a34, for the use of *to aoriston; An post.* 97b7; *Rhetoric* 1373a33). See also Sextus, *PI*, 1.198–9, where Sextus refers to the Pyrrhonian slogan that '*panta aorista*', 'all things are undefined'. There are other sources reporting Pyrrho's view that 'nothing is in itself honourable or shameful, just or unjust' (Diogenes Laertius 9.61=T1A Decleva Caizzi) or that 'there is nothing that by nature is good or bad' (S.E., *M.* 11.140). On the distinction between Pyrrho's use of *adiáphora* in this passage and the ethical usage of the same term by the Stoics, see Bett (2000, p. 28, n. 31) and Decleva Caizzi (1981, pp. 223–4).

'*Astáthmeta*' means 'unstable', 'unbalanced'. Decleva Caizzi lists some sources before Pyrrho, where the adjective has this meaning (Decleva Caizzi 1981, p. 224). The idea here is that things, again either in themselves or from an epistemological point of view, are unstable because they are trapped into a continuous and disordered movement: see *Tht.* 156a–157c, on which more later; Beckwith (2015, pp. 29–30) for similarities with the Sanskrit term '*duhkha*'.

'*Anepíkrita*' means 'undecided', again with the idea that things, either in themselves or in relation to our knowledge of them, cannot be determined – so that they are indeterminate. The adjective has no occurrences before Pyrrho's time and so some scholars regard it as one of Timon's neologisms (Chiesara 2001, p. 95). As it has been noted by Decleva Caizzi (1981, p. 225), the last of the three adjectives highlights the transition from the first of Pyrrho's question (about the nature of things) to the second, namely how the nature of things impacts on our epistemological activities.

4 The metaphysical reading has been defended by the following scholars: Berti (1981), Ferrari (1981), Reale (1981), Decleva Caizzi (1981), Long and Sedley (1987) and, more forcefully, by Bett (2000). Contrarily, the main defenders of the epistemological reading have been Stough (1969), Ausland (1989) and Brunschwig (1994), all going back to Zeller (1919–23). See also more recently Brennan (2008) and Greene (2017). It is worth highlighting that some of the contributions often quoted in this chapter are originally included in the two volumes on ancient scepticism edited by G. Giannantoni in 1981 (see Giannantoni 1981), which helped setting up a fresh debate on ancient scepticism. Stopper (1983: aka Jonathan Barnes under a pen name) is a critical review ('Schizzi pirroniani') of these two volumes.

5 The most sophisticated alternative account of the Aristocles passage is developed by Jacques Brunschwig in Brunschwig (1994); see also Brennan (2008) and

Greene (2017), on which more below. In his chapter, Brunschwig brings about an attempt to distinguish in Aristocles' passage what is according to him genuinely Pyrrhonian material from what is due to Timon's intervention. In Brunschwig's interpretation, Timon is responsible for what he calls the 'epistemological swerve' in Aristocles' passage (thus making Timon the first truly sceptical Pyrrhonist in the history of thought), while he makes Pyrrho an ethicist primarily interested in the art of living. Overall, Brunschwig's account must be resisted for several reasons, including the ones I am about to formulate in this chapter's main text.

6   Greene (2017, p. 362) has recently challenged this point. I shall respond to his argument in note 9 below.

7   The textual emendation was first proposed by Eduard Zeller (1919-23: iii/I 501, n. 4); others who adopted the emendation are Stough (1969, p. 17) and, most forcefully, Stopper (1983, pp. 274–5 and note 53 at p. 292; see also Brunschwig, 1994). Stopper's connotation of the logical move from **1a** to **1b** in the Aristocles passage (that is, from the fact that things are undifferentiated, unstable and indeterminate to the fact that for this reason our opinions neither tell the truth nor lie) as a 'zany inference' (p. 292, note 53) has been widely quoted in subsequent scholarship (see, more recently, Greene 2017). Stopper writes: 'The transmitted text is clear: since things are indifferent, for that reason (*dià toūto*) our sense are unreliable. But that is a zany inference, as a little reflexion will show (…). The inference should go the other way about, as it does in later scepticism. We should accept Zeller's [emendation], which restores sense and syntax at one blow (I am not assuming that Timon thought in the same way as later Pyrrhonists and then emending the text to suit that assumption: the received text is wholly puzzling as it stands, and the emendation is compelling without any such assumption)'. *Excusatio non petita, accusatio manifesta*: the transmitted text is *not* puzzling as it stands; the inference is *not* zany at all, as shown in the main text above; the emendation is deemed necessary by someone who, as Stopper seems to be doing, projects later Pyrrhonism back into Aristocles' passage for ideological reasons (see e.g. Beckwith 2015, 198).

8   See Bett (2000, pp. 25–7). See also Decleva Caizzi (1981, pp. 225–7); Chiesara (2001, pp. 97–8). For a positive view on the emendation, see Brennan (2008).

9   Against a long tradition of scholars who have adopted the emendation to make the epistemological reading a viable option to read Aristocles' text, Greene (2017) has argued, rather surprisingly, that the epistemological reading makes good sense of Aristocles' passage' even without any emendation to be put in place. He

also argues that the metaphysical reading does not offer a coherent interpretation of the Aristocles passage. While I find his argument for the latter claim rather nebulous, I do not think his claim that the epistemological reading makes sense even without the emendation is convincing either. To make the epistemological reading an interpretation of Aristocles' text more plausible than the metaphysical reading, Greene makes some theoretical assumptions that, I believe, are not allowed by the text itself (see especially what he says at p. 362). On similar lines to Greene's, Brennan (2008) argues that to make good sense of the Aristocles passage, both the epistemological and the metaphysical reading need to make some philosophical assumptions that are unwarranted by the logic of the text. So, he adds, only by looking at the argumentative structure of the Aristocles' passage we are not able to grasp Pyrrho's views with enough confidence; we must thus look somewhere else, he concludes. To defend the epistemological reading as the most natural way to understand the Aristocles passage, Brennan reverts to the structure of Eusebius' account, which, he argues, is predominantly epistemological in tone. I reply to Brennan's argument by saying that I do not think that the metaphysical reading needs some further theoretical assumptions to make it intelligible as a plausible reading of Aristocles' text. At the same time, if we still need to look somewhere else to decide the real meaning of Aristocles' passage and, hence, Pyrrho's real views, why don't we look East, that is, at the affinities with some Buddhist views? This I do in the 'Pyrrho in India: Beckwith and Kuzminski' section.

10   Again, as in the answer (**1a**) to the first question about the nature of things (**1**), there is a list of three adjectives defining the right approach to take towards things once we have understood their nature. The three adjectives are again all in alpha-privative, as in **1a**: *adoxástous kaì aklineîs kaì akradántous*.

Adoxástous: literally it means 'with no opinions'. Notoriously, the problem of how a life with no beliefs is indeed possible is a central problem for scepticism: see Burnyeat (1997), Cavini (1981) and Perin (2010, chapter 4).

Aklineîs: see Plato, *Phd* 109a, where the term is applied to the Earth that, being at the centre of the Universe, does not incline towards anything because it is in perfect balance: see Decleva Caizzi 1981, p. 228.

Akradántous: from '*kràdē*', which is the actual end of a vibrating branch. The verb '*kradáō, – aínō*' means 'to shake', so that the adjective here means 'unshaken, not subject to any vibrations'. There is a semantic parallel in Timon's own description of the sceptic in S.E. M. 11.1 (=T61c Decleva Caizzi). Even for those scholars who believe in Timon's own intervention in Pyrrho's original views as these are illustrated in the Aristocles passage, the three adjectives characterizing the correct disposition towards things are authentically Pyrrhonian (see Brunschwig 1994, pp. 202–4).

Pyrrho himself has been often depicted in ancient sources as being *adoxástous kaì aklineîs kaì akradántous*: see Timon, TT61A,B,C,D Decleva Caizzi; Bett (2000, pp. 70–84), Beckwith (2015, pp. 48–55).

11 See Bett (2000, pp. 30–2); Decleva Caizzi (1981, pp. 228–30); against Stopper (1983, p. 274), where it is claimed that 'modern interpretations of Pyrrho (that is, those that challenge the traditional epistemological reading) are heresies to be anathematised'.

12 See Stopper (1983, p. 272); Bett (2000), Chiesara (2001, p. 103).

13 See Reale (1981, pp. 315–21) and Decleva Caizzi (1981, pp. 229–30). Against this reading (mainly refuting Reale's arguments), see Stopper (1983, pp. 272–5). See also Chiesara (2001, pp. 104–6). References to other sources that could confirm one of the two readings (such as Favorinus in Aulus Gellius=T56 Decleva Caizzi) are not decisive.

14 See Bett (2000, pp. 33–7); see also Beckwith (2015, pp. 202–3).

15 This point was first noticed by De Lacy (1958, pp. 59–71); see also Stopper (1983, p. 274).

16 Notoriously, the tetralemma is a key-feature of Buddhist logic and is also widely used in Sextus Empiricus: see e.g., *PH* 2.86–7. Frenkian (1957) and Flintoff (1980) both claim that Pyrrho discovered the tetralemma while conversing with the Naked Men during his trip to India. *Contra*, see Beckwith (2015, p. 40) and Bett (2000, pp. 171–8).

17 Again, as with the other two answers, we have here a list of two words beginning with alpha privative: *apahasía* and *ataraxía*. *Aphasia* is explained by Decleva Caizzi (1981, p. 231) as having a peculiar meaning in Pyrrho as the kind of speechlessness deriving from the lack of any emotional turmoil about things. On the contrary, see Bett (2000, pp. 38–9), which highlights how *apahasía* is often seen as deriving from fear or perplexity. The soteriological role of *ataraxía* as the final practical outcome of Pyrrho's views has been highlighted in comparative comparison with Buddhism: see Halkias (2020).

18 While *ataraxía* is a common target among Hellenistic schools, speechlessness is a rarer phenomenon to be met in post-Socratic philosophy. It is true that Sextus talks about *aphasía* in a section of the *Outlines of Pyrrhonism* (1.192–3) and, before him, in *Metaphysics* 4 Aristotle refers to speechlessness as the right attitude to take for those who deny the principle of non-contradiction. But to see *aphasia* as the result of someone endorsing Pyrrho's views seems to conflict with

what Pyrrho is said to have suggested in the preceding lines of the Aristocles passage, that is, that for each thing we should *say* that it no more is, than is not, or that both is and is not, or that neither is nor is not (yet, together with a new language more apt to capture the thread of reality, *aphasia* may become the most natural approach to adopt in the long run for someone endorsing metaphysical indeterminacy). For these reasons, Beckwith has suggested an emendation in the text, that is, to replace '*aphasía*' with '*apatheia*', 'passionless'. The two words are very similar in ancient Greek – this is even more so in the Doric Greek, he argues, which is both Pyrrho's and Timon's main dialect (see Beckwith 2015, pp. 206–10). While not directly proposing an emendation to the original text, Decleva Caizzi too (1981, pp. 232–3), highlights the ternary structure that is typical of Aristotle's passage, with *adiáphora kaì astáthmēta kaì anepíkrita* (as referred to things), paralleled by *adoxástous kaì aklineîs kaì akradántous* (as referred to our disposition towards things). In the transmitter text, the result for those who are without opinions, inclinations and wavering are two, not three: *aphasia* and *ataraxia*, thus lacking a third term, which again decleva Caizzi suggests could have been *apatheia*. For other possible reasons why pleasure is inserted as a third outcome, see Chiesara (2001, pp. 107–8).

19 See Bett (2000, pp. 152–60): despite recognizing an ethical linkage between atomism and Pyrrho's views, he plays down any possible metaphysical influence of Democritus' atomism on Pyrrho. See also his criticism of Decleva Caizzi's view of Pyrrho's possible fascination with atomism (Bett 2000, pp. 187–8, arguing against Decleva Caizzi 1984). On the ethical linkage between ancient atomism and Pyrrho, see, most notably, Warren (2002, chapter 4); for a more positive view of Democritus' metaphysical influence on Pyrrho, see Kuzminski (2021).

20 As he puts it (Bett 2000, pp. 116–17): 'in order to yield the indeterminacy thesis, the reasoning would somehow have to run along the following lines: things present themselves to us in various and conflicting ways; so there is no single, fixed way things are; so reality is indeterminate'. Against, see Greene (2017, p. 347).

21 See Bett (2000, pp. 123–32), where it is argued that while reflecting the importance of ontological variability in Presocratic and Socratic philosophy, Aristotle's discussion has little to do with Pyrrho's indeterminacy thesis. *Contra*, Decleva Caizzi (1981, pp. 226), Zilioli (2013b).

22 According to Sextus, Anaxarchus 'likened existing things to a scene-painting and supposed them to resemble the impressions experienced in sleep or madness'

(M. 7.88). On this view of Anaxarchus, see Burnyeat (2017); for the possible conceptual linkage between Pyrrho's indeterminacy thesis and Anaxarchus' view, see Bett (2000, pp. 162–4).

23 See *R.* 479a–c; *Tht.* 182e and 183b (the latter passages were already highlighted by Decleva Caizzi 1981, p. 242).

24 Bett's main reason for rejecting any direct influence on Pyrrho on the part of the Naked Men during his trip to India is the impossibility of communicating directly by means of a shared, common language. The sophistication of the philosophical views being discussed should have required – he argues – very competent interpreters, versed in both philosophical traditions. This, Bett claims, is highly unlikely (Bett 2000, pp. 177–8). This seems to me a weak argument for excluding any substantial philosophical exchange between Pyrrho and the Indian thinkers (see e.g., Stoneman 2021, p. 351). Much before Pyrrho, Herodotus travelled far and wide, meeting a variety of people whose languages were unknown to him and he managed to understand them by relying on qualified interpreters. There are nine books of his *Histories* to witness the very possibility of inter-linguistic/cultural dialogue well before Pyrrho.

25 Much of what is available as historical evidence of Pyrrho's trip to India as well as on the cultural and philosophical climate that he may have found there can be read in Beckwith (2015, pp. 5–21, 61–137).

26 Beckwith (2015, p. 23); see also Appendix A (*Classical sources on Pyrrho*), which appeared as a self-standing research chapter in *Elenchos* 2011 ('Pyrrhos' Logic': issue 2; pp. 287–327).

27 Beckwith stretches his case too much when he takes '*pragmata*' to refer to ethical matters only. The term has a much wider meaning in ancient Greek and it does principally refer to material objects or events in the world. The same critical remark applies to the way he understands the term '*dharma*' too in Sanskrit (again with the term having a much wider meaning than Beckwith allows for: see above, pp. 37 ff.). See both entries in the LSJ and the Monnier-Williams. See also Kuzminski (2021, pp. 17–18 and 77ff), where '*pragma*' is taken to imply 'dependently originated' and is seen as broadly equivalent to '*dharma*'.

28 The three key-terms of '*anitya*', '*duhkha*' and '*anātman*' are further glossed by Beckwith at pp. 29–34. It is worth noticing that Beckwith reverses the order of correspondence between the three adjectives in the Aristocles passage and those in the *Trilaksana*. According to Beckwith, the list of pairing adjectives are the following ones: *anitya* with *anepíkrita*, *duhkha* with *astáthmēta* and *anātman* with *adiáphora*. On Beckwith's analysis of these three adjectives, see the

critical remarks of Goodman (Goodman 2018), and Beckwith's further reply (Beckwith 2018).

29 On early Buddhism, see Gombrich (2011). Another innovative claim made by Beckwith is that Buddha was originally a Scythian reacting to Zoroastrianism, not Brahmanism, thus locating the area where Buddha lived and practised much closer to mainland Greece than usually thought of (see Beckwith 2015, pp. 5–13).

30 See also Beckwith (2015, Appendix 2).

31 Beckwith's book has ignited a fierce debate about some of its main innovative claims: see Johnson and Shults (2018), Kuzminski (2018), Goodman (2018) and some replies by Beckwith (2018), all the last three exchanges in *Philosophy East and West*.

32 See also Kuzminski (2021, p. 14): 'Imagine how Pyrrho, armed as a young man with the atomistic insights of Leucippus, Democritus and Anaxarchus, might think about the phenomenalism he encountered among early Buddhists. For Democritus and his tradition, atoms were believed to be imperceptible, impenetrable items moving through the void. What Pyrrho might well have done, in trying to understand Buddhism with the mindset of a Greek atomist, is to recognize that the phenomena present to consciousness for Buddhists were in fact the real atoms, very different from the fictional Democritian atoms. In Buddhism, it was not a question of imagined, imperceptible, impenetrable items moving in the void, as with Democritus, but of actual, perceptible thoughts and sensations moving in the stream of consciousness, endlessly combining and recombining as the facts, or *pragmata*, as Sextus puts it, which we experience'.

33 It is worth noticing that both Beckwith's and Kuzminski's reading draw important ethical and epistemological consequences from Pyrrho's metaphysical views, as does any reasonable attempt to interpret Pyrrho's philosophy as a complex and subtle philosophical approach. For our purposes here, these epistemological and ethical consequences need be set aside.

34 If not for very brief remarks by Decleva Caizzi (1981, p. 240), where she comments on another source on Pyrrho (Diogenes Laertius 9.105=T55 Decleva Caizzi), not on the Aristocles passage.

35 Protagoras' Secret Doctrine is first illustrated at *Tht.* 152d2–8, with the two accounts of perception deriving from that Secret Doctrine dealt with later: *Tht.* 153d8–154b9 and 156a–157c. Again, see mainly Chapter 1 for the four stages through which the Secret Doctrine is built out.

36 See *Tht.* 156a–157c and above, pp. 20–4.

37 On Pyrrho and metaphysical indeterminacy, see also Chapter 5, p. 88.
38 A similar view is held by McEvilley (2002, p. 495), although he is not specifically concerned with a metaphysical parallelism between Pyrrho and Buddhism.

Chapter 5

1   On Aristippus and early Cyrenaicism, see Giannatoni (1958); on the later sects, see Lampe (2014a); on a general historical introduction to early and late Cyrenaicism, see Zilioli (2012).
2   See Bett (2015) and O'Keefe (2015).
3   I champion O'Keefe (2013) and, more essentially, O'Keefe (2015) for the sceptical interpretation I aim to resist; see also Warren (2013). O'Keefe (2011) is an interesting attempt to highlight the different epistemological commitments of Pyrrhonists and Cyrenaics.
4   Unless otherwise stated, all translations of Cyrenaic sources are my own and are taken from the Appendix 'Cyrenaic testimonies in translation', to be found in Zilioli (2012, pp. 185–96). I often supply the appropriate reference to the canonical work of Giannantoni on the Socratics: *Socratis et Socraticorum Reliquiae*, Naples 1990 (*SSR*).
5   I do not take any position in the recent debate, triggered by Casin (2010), whether the sceptic has to believe what appears to him (a blatant case of Moore's paradox), since this is not immediately relevant to my own characterization of the term 'sceptic' here.
6   On the passage, see O'Keefe (2015). Although the term has wide circulation in Hellenistic philosophy, Klaus Döring has founded a first occurrence of the verb '*katalambano*' in the *Phaedrus* (250d1), hence allowing the possibility that in the account of Cyrenaic philosophy he provides us with Sextus actually reports the original Cyrenaic position *ipsissima verba:* Doring (1988, p. 29).
7   Lee (2010, p. 22).
8   See above, pp. 15–6.
9   On the connection between eliminativism, indeterminacy and nihilism, see the Conclusion.
10 Tsouna (1998, p. 82, see also 75–88).
11 Zilioli (2012, pp. 76–83).
12 Both Bett (2015) and O'Keefe (2015) highlight the overt epistemological tone of Sextus' passage (and of other passages dealing with the Cyrenaics, such as Plutarch, Cicero, Aristocles). In interpreting Sextus' passage (and others) as committing the

Cyrenaics to metaphysical indeterminacy, I do not want to deny the epistemological flavour of those sources. Rather, I aim to emphasize that a metaphysical reading of some sections or lines of those passages is also available (or at least possible), even if the epistemological tone in those passages looks preponderant. In the prosecution of Sextus' passage (*M.* VII 194, quoted), the sentence 'what is external and productive of the affection perhaps is a being, but it is not a *phainomenon* for us' is a clear example of the metaphysical reading I have in mind. On the other hand, as far as Sextus' reliability as a source is concerned, the overt epistemological tone of his main report on the Cyrenaics (*M.* VII 191–200) too often betrays a technical jargon (such as the talk of places, distances, motion, changes and so on at *M.* VII 195) and is likely to be due to Sextus' genuinely sceptical approach.

13 O'Keefe (2015, p. 155) objects to me that I take '*huparchein*' in Sextus' passage in a too particular sense, i.e. implying that 'sound (alongside everything other than the *pathê*) does not exist as a proper or determinate being, while allowing that it exists indeterminately'. I take my reading of '*huparchein*' in Sextus' passage to be plausible. In addition I well accept Harold Tarrant's (in Tarrant 2014, p. 127) that, to make my indeterminacy case stronger, I should have ventured to translate '*huparchein*' in Sextus' passage as 'to be present [to one]'. Both Bett (2015) and O'Keefe (2015) warn me that my reading of Sextus' passage does not seem to help the case of indeterminacy, since the passage is taken to deny that anything other than affections really exists. As Bett puts it: 'if there is really *nothing* beyond the *pathê*, there is not even an indeterminate reality' (Bett 2015, p. 261). Let me briefly recapitulate my reading of Sextus' passage on sound for the sake of clarity. On my interpretation, Sextus attributes to the Cyrenaics the following view: only *pathê* exist, what causes them does not. On this understanding, sound (that is, a material item like chairs and tables) does not (properly) exist. And this type of not-existence can be interpreted as a commitment to metaphysical indeterminacy exactly in light of what I have shown at pp. 87–88 in the 'Metaphysical indeterminacy' section of this chapter.

14 Sextus' passage goes on like this: 'By denying the existence of every sensory object [*aisthēton*], the schools of Democritus and Plato deny the existence of sound as well, for sound is a sensory object'. Following Tsouna (1998, p. 80), O'Keefe (2015) suggests that in the passage on sound Sextus is not concerned with historical accuracy in reporting the view of the Cyrenaics, since he attributes the same (untenable) view to Plato and Democritus. On my part, I am happy to recognize the dialectical context in which Sextus puts the passage on sound. I am not inclined, however, to take the views reported by him in that passage as

a pure dialectical game to attack the implicit belief of the professors of art and music in the existence of sound. In effect, to disregard the philosophical content of Sextus' passage on sound simply in light of the dialectical context in which he puts it would be tantamount to distrusting Sextus' main report on the Cyrenaics (that is, *M.* VII 191–200) because in that report Sextus betrays too often his sceptical approach in reporting the views of the Cyrenaics. In short, although he puts it in a dialectical context, the view on sound Sextus attributes to the Cyrenaics needs to be taken seriously. In addition, the attribution of the same view to Democritus and Plato need not be understood simply as a polemical concession in the dialectical context of the passage. In attributing to Democritus and Plato that view, Sextus may have had in mind Protagoras' Secret Doctrine as this is sketched out of Plato's *Theaetetus*, where as shown in Chapter 1 the subtler thinkers are made to argue that material items (such as sound) do not exist, since the world is just a dialectical process between active and passive powers.

15 O'Keefe (2015, p. 156) objects to me that I read this passage, as the one on sound in Sextus, in terms of types of existence and not, as he does, in terms of mere existence. In addition, he notes that, even if my reading of it is plausible, the passage itself will not support my metaphysical indeterminacy thesis, since in the passage 'the Cyrenaics are asserting that we *cannot know* about the being of external things, rather than asserting that external things *are not* proper beings'. I reply to O'Keefe by saying that I do not deny that Sextus' passage has mainly an epistemological concern. Yet, the very final line of the passage 'What is external and productive of the affection [*to d'ektos kai tou pathous poiētikon*] perhaps is a being [*tacha men estin on*]' well allows for a metaphysical reading, and one that interprets the mere denial of being for what is external to the percipient as a commitment to a radical form of metaphysical indeterminacy.

16 My translation modified, following the suggestion of Kechagia (2011), pp. 253–4. On this passage, see also Chapter 6, pp. 104–5.

17 Another passage of Aristocles on the Cyrenaics (Eusebius, *PE* 14.19.1–3) is susceptible to be interpreted along the two philosophical alternatives I am here discussing. Again, see Chapter 6, pp. 106–8.

18 See Tsouna (1998), p. 83; Kechagia (2011), pp. 260, 264. O'Keefe (2015) labels the second option as 'object identity skepticism'. Against Warren (2013), O'Keefe argues that Colotes' argument commits the Cyrenaics to 'object identity skepticism'. I agree with him on this overall reading of Colotes' passage (although in footnote 5, p. 171, he seems to imply that our reading of the passage differs).

What I ultimately disagree him with is whether 'object identity skepticism' leads to what he calls 'global object identity skepticism', the idea that, as he puts it, 'this object identity skepticism extends to the structure of the world in general' (O'Keefe 2015, p. 167). Since O'Keefe's 'global object identity skepticism' is something very close to what I call 'metaphysical indeterminacy', rather unsurprisingly I think that 'object identity skepticism' leads quite naturally to 'global object identity skepticism', whereas O'Keefe thinks that, given the evidence, we should suspend our judgement on the question.

19 Plutarch, *Against Colotes* 1120e–f.
20 According to Aristotle, those who deny the principle of non-contradiction 'seem (…) to be stating something indeterminate (*to aoriston*)' (4.5.1007b27–8). He also says that those who believe that all appearances are true deny the principle of non-contradiction because 'they believed that things-that-are are merely perceptibles; and in these things the nature of indeterminacy [*he tou aristou phusis*] is an important constituent' (1010a3–4).
21 For an alternative reading of Colotes' passage, see Warren (2013).
22 See Chapter 1, pp. 14–5.
23 A similar view is ascribed by the Anonymous to the followers of Pyrrho: 'the Pyrrhonists say that everything is relative, inasmuch as nothing exists in its own right but everything is relative to other things. Neither shape nor sounds nor objects of taste and smell or touch nor any other object of perception has an intrinsic character on its own' (col. LXIII, 3–11). On this passage, see Conclusion.
24 In Zilioli (2013a), in line with attempts further back in time (Grote and Zeller), I make a case for identifying the subtler thinkers of the *Theaetetus* (at 156a3) with the Cyrenaics. Chapter 1, see also above, p. 130, note 10.
25 While O'Keefe (2015) does not comment on this passage as a possible source for committing the Cyrenaics to metaphysical indeterminacy, Bett (2015) warns me not to take the Anonymous' report too seriously because it looks as internally inconsistent. The quality and perspicuity of the Anonymous' commentary has often been disputed but the general view among scholars nowadays is that it is rather insightful on many passages of Plato's *Theaetetus*. At the same time, I do not see any inconsistency on the Anonymous' passage on the Cyrenaics: he may have been inaccurate in using '*adelon*' when referring to the causticity of the fire, but I find his overall argument quite straightforward.
26 Indelli and Tsouna (1995), *ad locum* and (1998, pp. 146–7).
27 See, e.g., DL II 85.
28 There is here a conceptual linkage between emptiness and indeterminacy that sounds close to Nāgārjuna's views.

29 Tsouna-Indelli, *ad locum*; Winiarczyk (1981), pp. 44–5 (T 66 on Theodorus) and Dorandi (2015). While agreeing with me that Philodemus' passage refers to the Cyrenaics, both O'Keefe (2015) and Bett (2015) object that the attribution of 'the manifest indeterminacy [of things]' is made with reference to 'others', hence not to the Cyrenaics. The objection does not hold, I think, for the reason that 'others' does refer to the Cyrenaics, that is, to a later sect of the school. Philodemus mentions 'others' because in the passage he is likely to be dealing with all the different sects of the Cyrenaic school, since his aim is to offer an exhaustive assessment of Cyrenaic philosophy as a whole (in Zilioli (2012, chapter 8), I have shown the substantial doctrinal continuity among all those Cyrenaic sects; contra, see Lampe 2014a).
30 O'Keefe (2015) for the sceptical interpretation of the Cyrenaic jargon.
31 Elsewhere (Zilioli 2012), in particular chapters 5–7, I have argued that an appeal to metaphysical indeterminacy helps answering these questions for the Cyrenaics, as well as explaining some other important aspects of their philosophy (in particular, of their philosophy of language) that, if explained along the traditional lines, would otherwise be completely inexplicable.
32 See Bett (2015). Although he thinks that a 'sizeable portion of the evidence for the Cyrenaic position is compatible with Zilioli's interpretation', he concludes that 'the traditional interpretation of the Cyrenaics as focused on out lack of knowledge of anything beyond the pathê is after all correct' (p. 113).

Chapter 6

1 See the references quoted above Introduction, p. 129, note 18.
2 On Aristocles' passage on the Cyrenaics, see below, pp. 106–8: the 'Cyrenaic solipsism II: Aristocles of Messene' section.
3 See Chapter 5, pp. 97–99 and below, pp. 110–2.
4 As Sextus Empiricus puts it when he deals with the Cyrenaics: 'One cannot grasp the affection of the neighbours nor can his neighbour, since he cannot feel the affection of that other person" (Sextus, M. 7.196).
5 Pihlström (2020).
6 Langton (2009).
7 *Contra*, see Tsouna (1998, pp. 96–104).
8 Again, see Pihlstrom (2020) for a very rich and informed overview of the varieties of solipsism.

9   It is worth noting that the sort of solipsism that is described in the two quotations is a combination of epistemological and existential/metaphysical views. Philstrom (2020, p. 24) labels this sort of solipsism as 'classical solipsism'. He writes: 'If the metaphysical dimension of this doctrine (sc. classical solipsism) is emphasised, classical solipsism claims that my experiences exhaust reality; if the epistemological dimension is taken to be central, the claim is rather that I cannot know (certainly, at last), or even justifiably believes, that they don't'.
10 All translations are my own.
11 See e.g., S.E. *M.* 7. 191–2; see below, pp. 110–2.
12 On the Cyrenaics as being unaware of what is actually affecting them, see also *The Anonymous Commentary on Plato's* Theaetetus, col. 65.29–39 (expanding on *Tht.* 152b), on which see Chapter 5, p. 94.
13 As Chiesara points out (Chiesara 2001, p. 139), Aristocles has surely in mind here the crucial section of Plato's *Theaetetus* on which we have focussed in Chapter 1: see above, especially pp. 20–4.
14 For the less encompassing charge of *apraxia* as levelled against the Cyrenaics, see Zilioli (2016).
15 Sedley (2018, p. 64). On internal touch in Cyrenaic thought, see also Tsouna (1998, pp. 18–20, 44–5) and Zilioli (2012, pp. 125–8).
16 On solipsism in Buddhist philosophy, see the works by Dharmakīrti and Ratnakīrti quoted above: Introduction, p. 7.
17 There are some textual problems for the things to which the *onomata* are supposed to apply in 7.195: '*chrêmasin*' is adopted by Natorp and Mannebach, while Kayser has '*pragmasin*' (thus duplicating 7.198), Bekker '*krimasin*', Mutschmann and Giannantoni '*synkrimasin*'. As Tsouna has noted (1998, pp. 106–7), all these terms can either refer to 'external objects' or to *pathê*. It is clear from the context of Sextus' passage however that the main problem for the Cyrenaics is how common names refer to private affections.
18 As Todd says, the solipsist should coherently maintain that 'everything which can ordinarily be said could, in theory, be said in a language which referred to one's own sensations (i.e. a private language)' (Todd 1968, p. 24).
19 Tsouna has highlighted that the Cyrenaics could well belong to the lively conventionalist strand in the ancient philosophy of language: Tsouna (1998, p. 107).
20 On Wittgenstein's solipsism, see Hacker (1972, pp. 58–85, 185–214); Pears (1987, pp. 153–90); (1988, Part III, chapters 11 and 12); (2008, pp. 96–127); Philström (2020, pp. 64–80); Dionigi (2001, pp. 429–75).

21 Ayer (1966, p. 254).
22 See also *PI*, §244, 245, and, most meaningfully, § 261 and §404.
23 See e.g., *PI* §§261–3.
24 The first port of call for the private language argument is McGinn (2013), pp. 134–215 (with further references). See also Dionigi (2001, chapter 8), which scrutinizes a very large portion of secondary literature. A classical reading is, notoriously, Kripke (1984), which has sparked a great deal of debate.
25 It is worth noting that in his discussion of inner sensations Wittgenstein uses examples such as 'pain' and 'red' that actually belong to the same class of ethical and epistemological affections that the Cyrenaics themselves, most consider: see e.g., *PI*, §§ 244–6, 250–1, § 253, § 263, § 271 (on pain); §§ 273–5; § 278; §§ 284–9 (on perceptions of colours). On Wittgenstein on sensations, see also Wittgenstein (1993).
26 There are two famous cases allowing for private languages for inner sensations in philosophy: one is Descartes (C. Adam and P. Tannery, *Oeuvres de Descartes*, Paris 1897–1910, 12 vols: VII, 71; IV 573–4; *Principles* I LXVIII) and the other is Locke (*An Essay Concerning Human Understanding*, Book II.xxxii.15; III.ii.2–6; III.ix.4–14; III.x.26). Both cases suffer philosophical defeats in light of Wittgenstein's arguments. This has been shown by Kenny for Descartes (Kenny 1966) and by Hacker for Locke (1972, pp. 224–42). Ayer has tried to rebut Wittgenstein's arguments on private languages, but he has too failed (Ayer 1966: see Rhees 1966 on Ayer's argument).
27 See Hacker (1975, pp. 222–6); Dionigi (2001, pp. 435–40) (with further references).
28 See also Dionigi (2001, pp. 448–52).
29 See, above all, § 246. See also §§ 253, 303, 404, 405, 408. Wittgenstein investigates the topic of knowledge/certainty at a fuller extent in *On Certainty*, on which see Coliva (2010) and Hamilton (2014).
30 Zilioli (2014, chapter 5).
31 Wittgenstein (1958, pp. 62–4).

Conclusion

1 McEvilley (2002, chapters 1 and 14) provide us with an overview of the historical connections between Greece, India and the East. More recently, Autieri and Cobb (2022) is an indispensable collection for anyone interested in the cultural

as well as historical exchanges between East and West in Hellenism. Beckwith (2023) focuses on the Scythians as an important trait d'union between Greece, India and China in pre-Hellenistic and Hellenistic times.

2   See Chapter 4, p. 63.
3   See Introduction, p. 3.
4   See above, Chapter 3, p. 137, note 31.
5   On the Heart Sutra, see Kerr (2022) and Red Pine (2005).
6   See Section 2 in Kerr's edition.
7   On this idea, see recently Chien-Hsing Ho (2022), who advances a carefully crafted argument to show that radical indeterminacy is a view coherent in itself as well as deeply connected to Madhyamaka philosophy. I thank the Reviewer for the Press for this reference as well as for some suggestions that have helped me shape the final part of this Conclusion.
8   On this point, see the work by Alan Sidelle, especially Sidelle (2022).
9   See Westerhoff (2020a), quoted in the *Introduction*, p. 127, n. 6.

References

Ancient Greek Philosophy

Ademollo, F. (2007), *The Cratylus of Plato. A Commentary*, Cambridge: Cambridge University Press.
Ausland, H. (1989), 'On the Moral Origin of Pyrrhonian Philosophy', *Elenchos* 10: 359–434.
Berti, E. (1981), 'La critica allo scetticismo nel libro IV della *Metafisica*', *Giannantoni* 1: 63–79.
Bett, R. (1994), 'Aristoteles on Timon on Pyrrho: The Text, Its Logic and Its Credibility', *Oxford Studies in Ancient Philosophy* 12: 363–81.
Bett, R. (2000), *Pyrrho, His Antecedents, His Legacy*, Oxford: Oxford University Press.
Bett, R. (2000a), 'Nietzsche on the Skeptics and Nietzsche as Skeptic', *Archiv Für Geschichte Der Philosophie* 82.1: 62–86.
Bett, R. (2015), 'Pyrrho and the Socratic Schools', in U. Zilioli (ed.), *From the Socratics to the Socratic Schools*, London and New York: Routledge, pp. 108–131.
Bett, R. (2020), 'Gorgias' *Peri tou me ontos* and Its Relation to Skepticism', *International Journal for the Study of Skepticism* 10: 187–208.
Brancacci, A. (2011), 'La dottrina riservata di Protagora (Plat. Theaetet. 152c7-e1)', *Methexis* 24: 87–108.
Brennan, T. (2008), 'Pyrrho on the Criterion', *Ancient Philosophy* 18: 417–34.
Brochard, V. (1887), *Les Sceptiques grecs*, Paris: Vrin.
Brunschwig, J. (1994), 'Once Again on Eusebius on Aristocles on Timon on Pyrrho', in *Papers in Hellenistic Philosophy*, Cambridge: Cambridge University Press, 190–211.
Buckels, C. (2016), 'The Ontology of the Secret Doctrine in Plato's *Theaeteus*', *Phronesis* 61.3: 243–59.
Burnyeat, F.M. (1982), 'Idealism in Greek Philosophy. What Descartes Saw and Berkeley Missed', *Philosophical Review* 91: 3–40.
Burnyeat, F.M. (1990), *The Theaetetus of Plato*, Indianapolis: Hackett.
Burnyeat, F.M. (1997), 'Can the Sceptic Live His Scepticism', in M. Burnyeat and M. Frede (eds.), *The Original Sceptics. A Controversy*, Indianapolis: Hackett, 25–57.
Burnyeat, F.M. (2017), 'All the World's a Stage Painting: Scenery, Optics and Greek Epistemology', *Oxford Studies Ancient Philosophy* 52: 33–77.

Campbell, L. (1861), *The Theaetetus of Plato*, Oxford: Clarendon. 1st edition, 2nd revised edition 1883.
Castagnoli, L. (2010), *Ancient Self-Refutation*, Cambridge: Cambridge University Press.
Cavini, W. (1981), 'Sesto Empirico e la logica dell'apparenza', in *Giannantoni* (1981), vol. 2: 533–46.
Chappell, S.G. (2020), 'Atoms, Complexes and Simples in the *Theaetetus*', in U. Zilioli (ed.), *Atomism in Philosophy*, London and New York: Bloomsbury, 112–36.
Chappell, T. (2005), *Reading Plato's Theaetetus*, Indianapolis: Hackett.
Chiesara, M.L. (2001), *Aristocles of Messene. Testimonia and Fragments*, Oxford: Oxford University Press.
Cornford, F.M. (1935), *Plato's Theory of Knowledge*, London: Routledge and Kegan Paul.
Corradi, M. (2012), *Protagora tra filologia e filosofia*, Roma-Pisa: Fabrizio Serra Editore.
Corti, A. (2014), *L'Adversus Colotem di Plutarco*, Leuven: Leuven University Press.
Day, J. (1997), 'The Theory of Perception in Plato's *Theaetetus*', *Oxford Studies in Ancient Philosophy* 15: 51–80.
Decleva, Caizzi (1981), *Pirrone. Testimonianze*, Naples: Bibliopolis.
Decleva, Caizzi (1984), 'Pirrone e Democrito. Gli atomi: un mito?', *Elenchos* 5: 5–23.
Decleva, Caizzi (2020), *Pirroniana*, Milan: Led.
De Lacy, P. (1958), '*Ou Mallon* and the Antecedents of Ancient Scepticism', *Phronesis* 3: 59–71.
Di Iulio, E. (2021), 'What Is Gorgias' "Not Being"? A Brief Journey through the Treatise, the Apology of Palamedes and the Encomium of Helen', *Archai* 31.
Di Iulio, E. (2022), *Gorgias' Thought. An Epistemological Reading*, London and New York: Routledge.
Dorandi, T. (2013), *Diogenes Laertius. Lives of Eminent Philosophers*, Cambridge: Cambridge University Press.
Dorandi, T. (2015), 'Epicureanism and Socraticism: The Evidence on the Minor Socratics from the Herculaneum Papyri', in U. Zilioli (ed.), *From the Socratics to the Socratic Schools*, London and New York: Routledge, 168–90.
Doring, K. (1988), *Der Sokratesschüler Aristipp und die Kyenaiker*, Mainz: Akademie der Wissenschaften und die Literature.
Everson, S. (1991), 'The Objective Appearance of Pyrrhonism', in S. Everson (ed.), *Psychology: Companions to Ancient Thought* 2. Cambridge: Cambridge University Press, 121–47.
Ferrari, G. (1981), 'L'immagine dell'equilibrio', *Giannantoni* (1981), vol. 2: 339–70.
Fine, G. (2003a), 'Sextus and External World Scepticism', in *Oxford Studies in Ancient Philosophy* 24: 341–85.
Fine, G. (2003b), 'Subjectivity, Ancient and Modern', in B. Inwood and J. Miller (eds.), *Hellenistic and Early Modern Philosophy*, Cambridge: Cambridge University Press, 192–230.

Fine, G. (2004), 'The Subjective Appearance of Cyrenaic Pathê', in V. Karasmanis (ed.), *Socrates: 2400 Years from His Death*, Delphi: European Cultural Centre of Delphi, 383–94.
Flintoff, E. (1980), 'Pyrrho and India', *Phronesis* 25: 88–108.
Frenkian, A. (1957), 'Sextus Empiricus and Indian Logic', *Philosophical Quarterly* 30: 115–26.
Giannantoni, G. (1958), *I Cirenaici*, Firenze: Sansoni.
Giannantoni, G. (ed.) (1981), *Lo Scetticismo antico*, 2 vols, Naples: Bibliopolis.
Gill, C. (2006), *The Structured Self*, Oxford: Oxford University Press.
Greene, J. (2017), 'Was Pyrrho a Pyrrhonian?', *Apeiron* 50: 335–65.
Indelli, G. and V. Tsouna. (1995), *Philodemus. On Choices and Avoidances,* Naples: Bibliopolis.
Ioli, R. (2010), *Gorgia di Lentini. Su ciò che non è*, Hildesheim-Zürich-New York: Olms.
Ioli, R. (2013), *Gorgia. Frammenti e Testimonianze*, Rome: Carocci.
Ioli, R. (2021), 'Between Eleatics and Atomists: Gorgias' Argument against Motion', *Archai* 31.
Irwin, T. (1991), 'Aristippus against Happiness', *The Monist* 74: 55–82.
Kechagia, E. (2011), *Plutarch against Colotes*, Oxford: Oxford University Press.
Keeling, E. (2018), 'Pathos in the *Theaetetus*', in L. Pitteloud and E. Keeling (eds.), *Psychology and Ontology in Plato*, New York: Springer, 55–66.
Laks, A. and G. Most (2016), *Early Greek Philosophy. Sophists. Part 1*, vol. VIII, Loeb Classical Library, Cambridge, MS: Harvard University Press.
Lampe, K. (2014a), *The Birth of Hedonism. The Cyrenaics and Pleasure as a Way of Life*, Princeton: Princeton University Press.
Lampe, K. (2014b), 'Review of Ugo Zilioli, *The Cyrenaics*,' *The Classical Review* 64: 53–6.
Lee, M.K. (2010), 'Antecedents in early Greek Philosophy,' in Richard Bett (ed.), *The Cambridge Companion to Ancient Scepticism*, Cambridge: Cambridge University Press, 13–35.
Long, A. and D. Sedley (eds.) (1987), *Hellenistic Philosophers*, 2 vols, Cambridge: Cambridge University Press.
Mazzara, G. (1999), *Gorgia. La Retorica del Verisimile*, Sankt Augustin: Academia.
Nemeth, A. (2017), *Epicurus on the Self*, London: Routledge.
O'Keefe, T. (2005), *Epicurus on Freedom*, Cambridge: Cambridge University Press.
O'Keefe, T. (2011), 'The Cyrenaics vs. the Pyrrhonists on Knowledge of Appearances,' in Diego Machuca (ed.), *New Essays on Ancient Pyrrhonism*, Leiden: Brill, 27–40.
O'Keefe, T. (2013), 'Review of Ugo Zilioli, *The Cyrenaics*,' *Notre Dame Philosophical Reviews*, November 4, 2013 (http://ndpr.nd.edu/news/39081-the-cyrenaics/).

O'Keefe, T. (2015), 'The Sources and Scope of Cyrenaic Scepticism', in U. Zilioli (ed.), *From the Socratics to the Socratic Schools*, London and New York: Routledge, 82–98.

Palmer, J. (2003), 'On the Alleged Incorporeality of What Is in Melissus', *Ancient Philosophy* 23: 1–10.

Pasnau, R. (2007), 'Democritus and Secondary Qualities', *Archiv fur Geschichte der Philosophie* 89: 99–121.

Perin, C. (2010), *Demands of Reason: An Essay on Pyrrhonian Scepticism*, Oxford: Oxford University Press.

Reale, G. (1981), 'Ipotesi per una rilettura della filosofia di Pirrone di Elide', *Giannantoni* (1981), vol. 1: 245–336.

Rodriguez, E. (2019), 'Untying the Gorgianic "Not": Argumentative Structure in On Not-Being', *Classical Quarterly* 69.1: 87–106.

Rossetti, L. (2017), 'Trilemmi: Il *PTMO* di Gorgia, tra Zenone e Melissa', *Peitho* 8: 155–72.

Rowe, C. (2015a), 'The First-Generation Socratics and the Socratic Schools: The Case of the Cyrenaics', in U. Zilioli (ed.), *From the Socratics to the Socratic Schools* London and New York: Routledge, 26–42.

Rowe, C. (2015b), *The Theaetetus and Sophist*, Cambridge: Cambridge University Press.

Sattler, B. (2020), *The Concept of Motion in Ancient Greek Thought*, Cambridge: Cambridge University Press.

Seaford, R. (ed.) (2017), *Universe and Inner Self in Early Indian and Early Greek Thought*, Edinburgh: EUP.

Sedley, D. (1983), 'Epicurus' Refutation of Determinism', in G. Pugliese Carratelli (ed.), *Studi sull'epicureismo greco e romano offerti a Marcello Gigante*, Naples: Macchiaroli, 11–51.

Sedley, D. (1988), 'Epicurean Anti-Reductionism', in J. Barnes and M. Mignucci (eds.), *Matter and Metaphysics*, Naples: Bibliopolis, 297–327.

Sedley, D. (2004), *The Midwife of Platonism*, Oxford: Oxford University Press.

Sedley, D. (2017), 'Zenonian Strategies', *Oxford Studies Ancient Philosophy* 53: 117–51.

Sedley, D. (2018), 'The Duality of Touch', in S. Purves (ed.), *Touch and Ancient Senses*, New York and London: Routledge, 64–74.

Sorabji, R. (2006), *Self*, Oxford: Oxford University Press.

Stoneman, R. (2019), *The Greek Experience of India*, Princeton: Princeton University Press.

Stopper, M.R. (1983), 'Schizzi Pirroniani', *Phronesis* 28: 265–97.

Stough, C. (1969), *Greek Scepticism*, Berkeley: University of California Press.

Tarrant, H. (2014), 'Review of Ugo Zilioli, *The Cyrenaics*', *Journal of the Platonic Tradition* 18: 126–8.

Thaler, N. (2013), 'Plato on the Importance of "This" and "That": The Theory of Flux and Its Refutation in the *Theaetetus*', *Oxford Studies in Ancient Philosophy* 45: 1–42.
Tsouna, V. (1998), *The Epistemology of the Cyrenaic School*, Cambridge: Cambridge University Press.
Warren, J. (2002), *Epicurus and Democritean Ethics. An Archeology of Ataraxia*, Cambridge: Cambridge University Press.
Warren, J. (2013), 'The Cyrenaics', in F. Sheffield and J. Warren (eds.), *Routledge Companion to Ancient Philosophy*, London and New York: Routledge, 409–22.
Winiarczyk, M. (1981), *Diagoras Melius Theodorus Cyrenaeus*, Leipzig: Teubner.
Zeller, E. (1919–23), *Die Philosophie der Griechen in ihrer geschichtlichen Entwicklung*, 3 vols, Leipzig: Reisland.
Zilioli, U. (2007), *Protagoras and the Challenge of Relativism. Plato's Subtlest Enemy*, Aldershot: Ashgate (reprinted for Routledge 2016).
Zilioli, U. (2012), *The Cyrenaics*, Durham: Acumen (1st edition); reprinted for Routledge 2014.
Zilioli, U. (2013a), 'The Wooden Horse: The Cyrenaics in the *Theaetetus*', in G. Boys-Stones, D. El Murr and C. Gill (eds.), *The Platonic Art of Philosophy*, Cambridge: Cambridge University Press, 114–32.
Zilioli, U. (2013b), 'Protagoras through Plato and Aristotle', in J.M. Ophuijsen, M. Van Raalte and P. Stork (eds.), *Protagoras of Abdera. The Man, His Measure*. Leiden: Brill, 233–58.
Zilioli, U. (ed.) (2015), *From the Socratics to the Socratic Schools. Classical Ethics, Epistemology and Metaphysics*, London and New York: Routledge.
Zilioli U. (2016), 'Could the Cyrenaics Live an Ethical Life?', in L. Corti and J. Vidal-Rosset (eds.), *Le scepticisme selon Jules Vuillemin, Philosophia Scientiae* 20: 29–48.

Buddhist Philosophy

Arnold, D. (2012), 'The Deceptive Simplicity of Nāgārjuna's Arguments against Motion: Another Look at *Mūlamadhyamakakārikā* Chapter 2', *Journal of Indian Philosophy* 40: 553–91.
Autieri, S. and M. Cobb (eds.) (2022), *Globalisation and Transculturality from Antiquity to the Pre-Modern World*, London and New York: Routledge.
Bareu, A. (2013), *The Buddhist Schools of the Small Vehicle*, Honolulu: University of Hawai Press.
Beckwith, C. (2015), *The Greek Buddha. Pyrrho's Encounter with Early Buddhism in Central Asia*, Princeton: Princeton University Press.

Beckwith, C. (2018), 'Early Buddhism and Incommensurability', *Philosophy East and West* 68: 1009–16.

Burton, D. (2014), *Emptiness Appraised. A Critical Study of Nāgārjuna's Philosophy*, London and New York: Routledge.

Carpenter, A. (2014), *Indian Buddhist Philosophy*, Durham: Acumen.

Carpenter (2015), 'Persons keeping their karma together', in Y. Deguchi, J. Garfield (eds), *The Moon points back*, Oxford: Oxford University Press, pp. 1–44.

Carpenter, A. (2020), 'Atoms and Orientation. Vasubandhu's Solution to the Problem of Contact', in U. Zilioli (ed.), *Atomism in Philosophy. A History from Antiquity to the Present*, London: Bloomsbury, 159–81.

Carpenter, A. (2023), 'Ethics of Atomism, or the Scepticism that wasn't', *British Journal History of Philosophy*.

Duerlinger, J. (2003), *Indian Buddhist Theories of Persons*, London: Routledge.

Duerlinger, J. (2013), *The Refutation of the Self in Indian Buddhism*, London: Roultedge.

Feldman and Philips. (2011), *Ratnakīrti's Proofs of Momentariness by Positive Correlation*, Berkeley: American Institute Buddhist Studies.

Frauwallner, E. (1951), *On the Date of the Buddhist Master of Law Vasubandhu*, Rome: ISMEO.

Galloway, B. (1987), 'Notes on Nāgārjuna and Zeno on Motion', *Journal of the International Association of Buddhist Studies* 10: 81–7.

Garfield, J. (1994), 'Dependant Co-origination and the Emptiness of Emptiness: Why Did Nāgārjuna Begin with Causation?', *Philosophy East and West* 44: 219–50.

Garfield, J. (1996), 'Emptiness and Positionlessness: Do Mādhyamika Relinquish All Views?', *Journal of Indian Philosophy and Religion* 1: 1–34.

Garfield, J. (2001), 'Nāgārjuna's Theory of Causation: Implications Sacred and Profane', *Philosophy East and West* 51: 507–24.

Gombrich, R. (2011), *How Buddhism Began: The Conditioned Genesis of the Early Teachings*, London and New York: Routledge.

Goodman, C. (2004), 'The Treasure of Metaphysics and the Physical World', *Philosophical Quarterly* 54: 389–401.

Goodman, C. (2018), 'Neither Scythian nor Greek: A Response to Beckwith's *Greek Buddha* and Kuzminski's 'Early Buddhism Reconsidered', *Philosophy East and West* 68: 984–1006.

Gowans, C. (2021), *Self-Cultivation Philosophies in Ancient India, Greece, and China*, Oxford: Oxford University Press.

Halkias, G. (2014), 'When the Greeks Converted the Buddha: Asymmetrical Transfer of Knowledge in Into-Greek Cultures', in P. Wick and V. Rabens (eds.), *Religion and Trade: Religious Formation, Transformation and Cross-cultural Exchange between East and West*, Leiden: Brill, 65–116.

Halkias, G. (2020), 'Yavanayāna: Buddhist Soteriology in the Aristocles Passage,' in O. Hanner (ed.), *Buddhism and Scepticism*, Hamburg: Numata Center for Buddhist Studies, 83–108.

Kapstein, M. (2001), 'Mereological Considerations in Vasubandhu's "Proof of Idealism"', in *Reason's Traces*, Boston: Wisdom, 181–204.

Kerr, A. (2022), *Finding the Heart Sutra*, London: Penguin.

Kim, W.D. (1999), *The Theravādin Doctrine of Momentariness*, Oxford: DPhil thesis.

Kritzer, R. (2003), '*Sautrāntika in the Abhidharmalośabhāsya*', Journal of the International Association of Buddhist Studies 26:2, pp. 331–84.

Kuzminski, A. (2018), 'Comment and Discussion: Early Buddhism Reconsidered', *Philosophy East and West* 68: 974–83.

Kuzminski, A. (2021), *Pyrrhonian Buddhism*, London and New York: Routledge.

Johnson, M.R. and B. Shults (2016), 'Early Pyrrhonism as a Sect of Buddhism? A Case Study in the Methodology of Comparative Philosophy', *Comparative Philosophy* 9: 1–40.

Lindtner, C. (1987), *Nagarjuniana, Studies in the Writings and Philosophy of Nāgārjuna*, Delhi: Motilal Banarsidass.

Mabbett, I. (1984), 'Nāgārjuna and Zeno on Motion', *Philosophy East and West* 34: 401–20.

Mabbett, I. (1998), 'The Problem of the Historical Nāgārjuna Revisited', *Journal of the American Oriental Society* 118: 332–46.

McEvilley, T. (2002), *The Shape of Ancient Thought. Comparative Studies in Greek and Indian philosophies*, New York: Allworth Press.

Priestly, L. (1999), *The Reality of the Indeterminate Self*, Toronto: University of Toronto Press.

Red Pine (2005), *The Heart Sutra*, Counterpoint LLC: Berkeley.

Ronkin, N. (2005), *Early Buddhist Metaphysics*, London and New York: Routledge.

Siderits, M. (2004), 'Causation and Emptiness in Early Madhyamika', *Journal of Indian Philosophy* 32: 393–419.

Siderits, M. (2016), *Personal Identity and Buddhist Philosophy. Empty Persons*, London and New York: Routledge.

Siderits, M. and D. O'Brien (1976), 'Zeno and Nāgārjuna on Motion', *Philosophy East and West* 26: 281–99.

Siderits, M. and S. Katsura (2013), *Nāgārjuna's Middle Way*, Somerville: Wisdom.

Stcherbatsky, T. (1922), *The Central Conception of Buddhism and the Meaning of the Word 'Dharma'*, London: Royal Asiatic Society.

Stoneman, R. (2021), *The Greek Experience of India*, Princeton: Princeton University Press.

Tola, F. and C. Dragonetti (1995), *On Voidness. A Study on Buddhist Nihilism*, Delhi: Motilal Banarsidass.

Tola, F. and C. Dragonetti (2004), *Being as Consciousness*, Delhi: Motilal Banarsidass.

Tucci, G. (1934), 'The Ratnāvalī of Nāgārjuna', *The Journal of the Royal Asiatic Society of Great Britain and Ireland* 2: 307–25.

Von Rospatt, A. (1995), *The Buddhist Doctrine of Momentariness*, Stuggart: Franz Steiner.

Warder, A.K. (1971), 'Dharmas and Data', *Journal of Indian Philosophy* 1: 272–95.

Westerhoff, J. (2008), 'Nāgārjuna's Arguments on Motion Revisited', *Journal of Indian Philosophy* 36: 455–79.

Westerhoff, J. (2009), *Nāgārjuna's Madhyamaka*, Oxford: Oxford University Press.

Westerhoff, J. (2010), *The Dispeller of Disputes*, Oxford: Oxford University Press.

Westerhoff, J. (2016), 'On the Nihilist Interpretation of Madhyamaka', *Journal of Indian Philosophy* 44: 337–76.

Westerhoff, J. (2018), *The Golden Age of Indian Buddhist Philosophy*, Oxford: Oxford University Press.

Westerhoff, J. (2020a), 'An Argument for Ontological Nihilism', *Inquiry* 64: 2–48.

Wood, T.E. (1991), *Mind Only*, Honolulu: University of Hawaii Press.

Wood, T.E. (1994), *Nāgārjunian Disputations. A Philosophical Journey through an Indian Looking Glass*, Honolulu: University of Hawaii Press.

Contemporary Philosophy

Ayer, A. (1966), 'Can There Be a Private Language?', in G. Pitcher (ed.), *Wittgenstein. The Philosophical Investigations*, London: Macmillan, 251–66.

Benovsky, J. (2018), *Eliminativism, Objects and Persons: The Virtue of Non-Existence*, London and New York: Routledge.

Bennett, K. and D.V. Zimmerman (eds.) (2011), *Oxford Studies in Metaphysics*, 6 Oxford: Oxford University Press.

Coliva, A. (2010), *Moore and Wittgenstein*, London: Palgrave.

Dionigi, R. (2001), *La fatica di descrivere. Itinerario di Wittgenstein nel linguaggio della filosofia*, Macerata: Quodlibet.

Hacker, P.M.S. (1972), *Insight and Illusion. Wittgenstein on Philosophy and the Metaphysics of Experience*, Oxford: Oxford University Press.

Hamilton, A. (2014), *Routledge Philosophy Guidebook to Wittgenstein and on Certainty*, London and New York: Routledge.

Ho, Chien-Hsing (2022), 'Can the World Be Indeterminate in All Respects?' *Ergo: An Open Access Journal of Philosophy* 9: 584–602.
Kenny, A. (1966), 'Cartesian Privacy', in G. Pitcher (ed.), *Wittgenstein. The Philosophical Investigations*, London: Macmillan, 352–70 (reprinted in many other places and collections).
Kim, J. (1993), *Supervenience and Mind. Selected Philosophical Essays*, Cambridge: Cambridge University Press.
Kripke, S. (1984), *Wittgenstein on Rules and Private Language: An Elementary Exposition*, Oxford: John Wiley.
Langton, R. (2009), 'Sexual Solipsism', in *Philosophical Essays on Pornography and Objectification*, Oxford: Oxford University Press.
Lewis, D. (1999), *Papers in Metaphysics and Epistemology*, Cambridge: Cambridge University Press.
Merricks, T. (2001), *Objects and Persons*, Oxford: Oxford University Press.
McGinn, M. (2013), *The Routledge Guidebook to Wittgenstein's Philosophical Investigations*, London and New York: Routledge.
Parfit, D. (1987), *Reasons and Persons*, Oxford: Oxford University Press.
Pears, D. (1987/8), *The False Prison. A Study of the Development of Wittgenstein's Philosophy*, 2 vols, Oxford: Clarendon.
Pears, D. (2008), *Paradox and Platitude in Wittgenstein's Philosophy*, Oxford and New York: Oxford University Press.
Philström, S. (2020), *Why Solipsism Matters*, London and New York: Bloomsbury Academic.
Rhees, R. (1966), 'Can There Be a Private Language?', in G. Pitcher (ed.), *Wittgenstein. The Philosophical Investigations*, London: Macmillan, 267–85.
Rosen, G. and J.J. Smith (2004), 'Worldly Indeterminacy: A Rough Guide', *Australasian Journal of Philosophy* 82: 185–98.
Rollins, C.D. (1967), 'Solipsism', in P. Edwards (ed.), *The Encyclopedia of Philosophy*, vol. 7, London: Macmillan, 487–91.
Sidelle, A. (2002), 'Is There a True Metaphysics of Material Objects?' *Noûs* 36.1: 118–45.
Simons, P. (2020), 'Atoms and Tropes', in U. Zilioli (ed.), *Atomism in Philosophy. A History from Antiquity to the Present*, London: Bloomsbury, 430–43.
Todd, W. (1968), *Analytical Solipsism*, The Hague: Nijhoff.
Unger, P. (2006a), 'There Are No Ordinary Things', in P. Unger (ed.), *Philosophical Papers* 2, Oxford: Oxford University Press, 3–36.
Unger, P. (2006b), 'Why There Are No People', in P. Unger (ed.), *Philosophical Papers* 2, Oxford: Oxford University Press, 53–112.
Van Inwagen, P. (1990), *Material Beings*, Ithaca: Cornell University Press.

Westerhoff, J. (2020b), *The Non-Existence of the Real World*, Oxford: Oxford University Press.

Wittgenstein, L. (1953), *Philosophical Investigations*, Oxford: Blackwell.

Wittgenstein, L. (1958), *The Blue and Brown Books*, Oxford: Blackwell.

Wittgenstein, L. (1993), 'Notes for Lectures on 'Private Experience' and 'Sense Data' and the Language of Sense Data and Private Experience (Notes by Rush Rhees)', in J. Klagge and A. Nordmann (eds.), *Philosophical Occasions, 1912–1951*, Indianapolis: Hackett.

Zilioli, U. (2020), *Atomism in Philosophy. From Antiquity to the Present*, London: Bloomsbury.

Index

Anonymous (MXG) 49–50, 53
Anonymous Commentary on the
    Theaetetus 94, 122–5
aphasia 72–5, 143–4
Aristocles passage (the) 66–75
    and the final outcome 72–5
    and the metaphysical/epistemological
        reading 67–72
    and the nature of things 70
    and our disposition towards things 70–2
Aristocles on the Cyrenaics 106–8
(Plutarch's) *Against Colotes*
    1120c-d: 91, 104
    1220e-f: 104–5

Beckwith, C. 63, 75–7, 78, 79, 138, 140,
    141, 143, 144–6, 154
Benovsky, J. 3, 127, 134
Bett, R. 27, 69, 71, 74–5, 78, 79, 99,
    131, 136, 139, 140, 144–5, 147, 148,
    150
Buckels, C. 9, 29, 33, 36, 43–5

Cicero's *Academica* 108–9
Cyrenaics (the) 83–4
    and the commonality of language
        109–11
    and indeterminacy 85–6, 94–7, 149,
        150–4
    and internal touch 108–9
    and the sceptical interpretation 84
    and solipsism 103–8, 112–17
    and privacy 115–17
    and their neologisms 97–99
    and Wittgenstein's private language
        argument 112–15

Dharmakīrti 7, 129, 152
Democritus 4–5, 63, 74, 77–8, 89, 119,
    128, 133, 144, 146, 148–9
dharmas 37–43, 76–7, 82, 133–4
    and the Secret Doctrine 41–3
    and tropes 39–41, 43–5

Gorgias' *On What Is not* 47–53
    and the Argument Generation and
        Eternity 49–51
    and the Argument against Monism
        and Plurality 52
    and the Argument against Motion 52–3
    and its structure 48–9
    and Nāgārjuna's arguments 55–61

Heart Sutra 123–4
Heraclitus 4–6, 25, 128
    and the Heracliteans 4, 75, 79, 81

indeterminacy 15–17, 24, 63, 87–8, 121–5, 129
    and the Cyrenaics 85–8, 90, 94–7, 149,
        150–4
    and Cyrenaic neologisms 97–99
    and nihilism 8, 122–5
    and Pyrrho 74–5, 79–81
    and the Secret Doctrine 15–17, 19, 24
    and things being also unstable and
        undifferentiated 67–70
    and the tetralemma 70–2

Kuzminski, A. 75, 77–9, 144, 145, 146

Merricks, T. 3, 5, 127
Mūlamadhyamakakārikā (*The Treatise on
    the Middle Way*)
    1:1: 56
    13:3: 60
    13:5: 60
    15:1–2: 56
    15:8: 57
    24:38: 60

Nāgārjuna's nihilist arguments 55–61
    and the Argument against Causation
        and Eternalism 55–7
    and the Argument against Change 59–61
    and the Argument against Plurality
        and Atomism 57–9
    and nihilism 54, 123–4

nihilism 47–8, 54, 60, 62–63
  and eliminativism 2, 122, 127, 134
  and emptiness 54, 136–7, 139
  and indeterminacy 8, 122–25
  and Nāgārjuna 54, 123–4
  and Pyrrho 63, 122–5

O'Keefe, T. 88, 128, 147–151

Parfit, D. 5–7, 128
Philodemus 94–7
(Protagoras') Secret Doctrine 15–24, 31–2, 41–3
  and Causal theory and phenomenalist interpretations 33–6
  and dharmas 41–3
  and indeterminacy 15–17, 19, 24
  and its stages 17–20, 21–4, 31–2
  and Pyrrho 78–81
  and swift/slow motions 31–3, 43–5
  and tropes 35–7, 43–5
  and a two-tier ontology 43–5
  and Vasubandhu 41–3
Pyrrho 63, 65–75, 81–2, 122–5
  and the Aristocles passage 66–75
  and early Buddhism 75–8
  and indeterminacy 74–5, 79–81
  and nihilism 63, 122–5
  and the Secret Doctrine 78–81
  and the tetralemma 71

Ratnakīrti 7, 129, 133, 152

Sedley. D. 33, 109, 128, 130, 134, 135, 136, 139, 152
selfhood 5–7
Sextus Empiricus
  M 6.53: 89
  M. 7.11: 85
  M. 7.68-72: 50–1
  M. 7.73-4: 53
  M. 7.191-2: 84
  M. 7.194: 90
  M. 195-8: 110
solipsism 101–8, 112–15
  and the Cyrenaics 103–8, 112–17
  and privacy 115–17
  and its varieties 102–3
  and Wittgenstein's private language argument 112–15
Stcherbatsky, T. 39–41, 133
Śūnyatāsaptakārikā (*The Seventy Stanzas on Emptiness*)
  3: 59
  21: 57
  32: 58
(Plato's) *Theaetetus* (see also the *Anonymous Commentary*)
  152d2-8: 15
  152d8-e1: 17
  153d8-a9: 18
  154a6-9: 19
  156a6-b7: 21, 30
  156c7-d2: 32
  156d3-e8: 22
  157a3-9: 22
  157a9-c2: 23
  183a2-6: 74
  183b1-5: 75, 79

Ratnāvalī (*The Precious Garland*)
  1:17: 58

tropes 35–7, 39–45
  and dharmas 39–41, 43–5
  and the Secret Doctrine 35–7, 43–5
  and a two-tier ontology 43–5
  and Vasubandhu's Treasury of Metaphysics 39–41
Tsouna, V. 88, 91, 94, 96, 128, 130, 148, 149, 150, 151, 152

Unger, P. 3, 127

Van Inwagen, P. 3, 5, 127
Vasubandhu's *Treasury of Metaphysics* 37–45
  1.43b: 132–3
  4.2b-3b: 39
  4.4: 37
  and dharmas 37–9

and tropes 39–41
and a two-tier ontology 43–5
and the Secret Doctrine 41–3

Westerhoff, J. 3, 40, 127, 129, 131, 132, 133, 134, 136, 137, 138, 154

Wittgenstein 112–17
  and the private language argument 112–15
  and solipsism 115–17
  and the *Philosophical Investigations* 112–15, 153